So You Want to Start a Mentorship Program

Nancy Kasmar
MS, SPHR, CCP

So You Want to Start a Mentorship Program is a reference for any SHRM chapter looking for a way to enhance the career development and professional growth of their chapter members. Based on a highly successful mentorship program, this book takes what could be an enormous start-up effort and packages it into an easy-to-follow process, reducing the work to a manageable level so you can begin your own successful mentorship program.

AFFILIATE OF

SOCIETY FOR HUMAN
RESOURCE MANAGEMENT

So You Want to Start a Mentorship Program

Copyright © 2014 by Lake Washington Human Resources Association (LWHRA), an affiliate of the Society for Human Resource Management (SHRM)

LWHRA
2150 N 107th St, Suite 205
Seattle, WA 98133
USA

Cover art copyright © Darrenw | Dreamstime.com - Helping Hand
Cover design and interior design copyright © 2014 by Knotted Road Press
www.KnottedRoadPress.com
"Why Mentor" artwork copyright © 2014 Breanna Trygg. Used with permission.

First edition December 2014
ISBN: 978-0-9847792-6-0

About the Author

Nancy Kasmar's journey into the world of HR was unconventional. After a career in nursing, Nancy applied her knack for relationships and mentoring to embrace a career in human resources. Following some expert advice, Nancy became a member of LWHRA and earned her SPHR certification. Later, while mastering the ins and outs of compensation consulting, Nancy earned her CCP designation.

Nancy herself was a mentee in 2008 when Warren Cohen, MS, SPHR, CPT, redesigned the LWHRA Mentorship Program. After Warren left his pioneering role, Nancy took on the role of mentorship program leader for the next three years. She served as the 2014 LWHRA President and continues to be involved with both LWHRA and the Washington State HR Council.

Acknowledgements

A chapter mentorship program was proposed to the LWHRA leadership more than a decade ago. The program goal was to support the chapter's mission of being a premier resource for members while advancing the profession. During its first few years the format was informal: individuals new to the HR profession were matched with a senior HR professional, a chapter member who volunteered their time to help a mentee acquire HR skills and knowledge to enhance their professional and personal growth. The informal format was successful, and several mentees had the opportunity to be mentored each year.

In 2008, one of the chapter leaders, Warren Cohen, devised a completely new approach for the mentorship program. His idea was to develop a formal mentorship program that created more structured opportunities for the mentees. He created both the program content and structure, standardized the length of the mentoring relationship, and chose to have everyone in the program act as a support group for each other. He also facilitated all the monthly meetings for the group for the first two years under the re-designed program.

Since that time, the mentorship program has evolved into a dynamic resource for both the chapter and its members. Over 100 mentor-mentee pairs participated in the program in the first seven years. Many people have contributed their time, ideas, and feedback to make the mentorship program the success it is today.

The 2013 board of directors had the original idea to write this book, and the 2014 board of directors reaffirmed their support to finish it. Their confidence that the book could and should be done kept me going through some tough times and deadlines. Big thanks go to Brent Schlosstein, Jennifer Richards, Carol Brickner, Donna Gray, Gayle Keenan, Josh Hedrick, Lindy Fowler, Sara Dnell, Nathan Deily, Shelley Fyfe, and Theresa Kinney. Thanks for believing in this book!

Thanks also goes to Alex Alonso, Vice President for Research at SHRM, for all his encouragement during the process of writing this book.

I'd also like to thank our publisher, Leah Cutter of Knotted Road Press. I am firmly convinced she knows *everything* about book publishing. And of course Anje Sandvik, the perfect editor, who knew exactly how to say what I intended, and tried her best to encourage good grammar. Any grammatical errors in the book are definitely mine.

Lastly, this book is dedicated to Warren Cohen, Karren Eckwortzel, Shannon Drohman, and all the mentors and mentees those who have been a part of the program since 2008. Thank you for your hard work, dedication, and caring. You made the mentorship program successful. It wouldn't be the same without you.

Respectfully,

Nancy

Nancy Kasmar, MS, SPHR, CCP
LWHRA President, 2014
LWHRA Mentor, 2011 - 2013
LWHRA Mentorship Program Chair, 2010 – 2012
LWHRA Mentee, 2008
www.linkedin.com/in/nancykasmar

Preface

Since 2008, over 100 LWHRA members have participated in the chapter's formal mentoring program. The program is extremely successful, with recognized benefits for both the individual participants and the chapter. Mentees use their participation in the mentorship program to develop their HR knowledge and skills. An informal network of current and past mentorship participants has developed to share best practices, HR knowledge, and employment opportunities.

For us, the mentorship program has become a way to discover and nurture emerging leaders within the chapter membership. Former mentorship program participants have become chapter volunteers, taking on roles of responsibility such as leading a committee or serving on the board of directors. A former mentee was chosen as Volunteer of the Year. Another was honored with the President's Cup Award for their volunteer service to the chapter. One of the first mentees in the program is currently chapter president. News about the mentorship program has spread within the local HR community, and the mentorship program has become a popular reason for local SHRM members to affiliate with LWHRA as their home chapter.

This book on how to start and run your mentorship program was created for other SHRM chapters who want to reap the benefits of starting their own mentorship program.

CONTENTS

WHY MENTOR?

Build community

Strengthen your association

Give back

Create Stars

Why Mentor At All?

It's a good idea before starting your mentorship program to figure out *why* to do it. It's a large time commitment on the part of the leader and the mentorship committee, so you need a compelling reason for people to invest that amount of time in starting a new program.

There are many, many ways a mentorship program benefits an organization. A fundamental reason to start a mentorship program is the desire to invest in the development of the emerging members of the profession. Channeling and using the collective wisdom of those more senior in the profession benefits all the participants as they progress in their career.

It is impossible to predict in advance what information provided or which relationship begun in a mentorship program will prove valuable in the years that follow. We do know that having a mentorship program benefits everyone who's a part of it. The mentees gain professional development and increase their professional network. The mentors develop their own network while sharing information about best practices. The program committee members have the opportunity to develop leadership skills. Lastly, the profession benefits when members advance sooner in their career with more time to apply their skills for the benefit of everyone around them.

In the words of one of our mentees:

"During my second year in HR my chapter started a mentorship program. When I saw the notice about it on our website, I applied immediately. HR is my second career, and I was excited about having the chance to be around someone who knew more about HR than I did. I also needed help with the tough situations in my very first HR job. There seemed to be a new challenge every day.

My goals for the mentorship program were straightforward: Finish my HR management certificate, take (and pass) the SPHR exam, and find a new job. I accomplished all my goals in the program in the first three months. What I didn't understand then was the value of the relationships between all the mentors and mentees in the program with me.

In the six years since my mentorship program ended, I have learned to appreciate the quality of the relationships I formed that year. Among many other things, I gained some lifelong friends. Several of the mentors that year are the people I go to with questions and for validation that I really do understand those tricky HR situations.

A year after I finished the program myself, I was given the opportunity to lead the mentorship program for the next three years. Seeing the value created in others' lives gave me even more appreciation for the positive impact the program has in the careers and lives of the participants. Even better, I can see that investing in the emerging HR professionals in our chapter allows them to contribute to others in turn.

I am grateful every day that I had the opportunity to participate in the mentorship program. I am very sure I would not have been able to accomplish everything I've done in the last six years without it." – N.L.K.

Why Use This Book

The purpose of this book is to provide you with a proven process to create your mentorship program. We started our mentorship program for two reasons: 1) to help our less experienced members advance in the HR profession, and 2) to create a way for our more experienced members to give back to the human resource management profession.

Our mentorship program began informally twelve years ago and grew from there. Today it is a structured, formal mentorship program lasting one year, with approximately fifteen mentor-mentee pairs participating each year. Over 100 mentor-mentee pairs have participated in the formal mentorship program, with outstanding results.

Many former mentees choose to volunteer on chapter committees and programs after their year in the mentorship program, and one of the first mentees is the currently the chapter president. Each year we literally see the chapter mission of furthering the ongoing enhancement of a dynamic, diverse membership unfold before us.

How to Use This Book

This book was written to help you start your chapter mentorship program so you can experience the increased benefits for your members and your chapter. Whatever your reason for starting your mentorship program, we hope you find useful guidance here.

Use this book as a way to begin your own process, and don't be surprised if you begin tweaking your mentorship program right away. If there is one thing we've learned over the years, it is that there really is "no one size fits all" when it comes to a program like this. So, start at the beginning and use what you think will work for your chapter.

Above all, *HAVE FUN!* That's the first rule of our mentorship program. It helps us decide what to keep, what to add, and what to stop doing as we start the planning process each year.

What's in This Book

A professional development tool. This book was written to share the collected knowledge of other HR professionals. Their stories and experiences related to developing a successful mentorship program are included to help you understand how the program and processes developed over time.

Step-by-step processes. This book breaks out the work necessary to start a mentorship program into steps and outlines the progression of activities within each step.

Tips for implementing your mentorship program. Throughout the book, we emphasize various notes and tips that will help you direct your efforts to the activities that will make your program successful.

A reference. The chapters are organized in chronological order so you and your mentorship committee can reference the steps and tips as you need them. An index is included to allow you to look up an activity or process quickly.

Templates for getting started. The appendix and download area contain samples and templates for you to use in the first year of your mentorship program.

Road Map

Chapter 1, *Mentorship Program Overview* describes the formulation process and steps to set up and run your mentorship program.

Chapter 2, *How To Begin* describes the planning process to start your mentorship program. Determining your goals and building a plan are the crucial first steps in creating a successful program.

Chapter 3, *Marketing* describes how to create a marketing plan and includes detailed strategies for finding and attracting applicants for your mentorship program.

Chapter 4, *Participant Selection* provides step-by-step guidance for conducting the application process and selecting your program participants.

Chapter 5, *Speed Mentoring* provides step-by-step guidance for conducting the speed mentoring meeting and matching your mentor-mentee pairs.

Chapter 6, *Training* describes how to orient the program participants around the structure and methodology of your mentorship program.

Chapter 7, *Monthly Program Meetings* covers the nuts and bolts of conducting the mentorship program meetings. This chapter discusses in detail coordinating and facilitating the program meetings, and monitoring the progress of the mentor-mentee pairs throughout the program.

Chapter 8, *Program Completion* discusses how to end your mentorship program and celebrate the successes of the program and its participants. It also includes information on discovering lessons learned from the mentorship program and incorporating those lessons in next year's program.

Chapter 9, *Key Learnings* contains information that bears repeating due to its critical role in our mentorship program. It is positioned here to be sure you have one more chance to review some of the drivers of success for your mentorship program.

Chapter 10, *In Their Own Words* contains testimonials from previous mentorship program participants about the benefits they received from being a part of our mentorship program.

Additional Resources

Appendices. Contains samples of the documents and supplemental information referenced in the book.

Glossary. A collection of the key terms used throughout this book, with a brief definition of each term.

Index. A list of topics discussed in the book with the page number where you can find the information.

Chapter 1
MENTORSHIP PROGRAM OVERVIEW

It helps to lay the groundwork for your first mentorship program the year before you actually want to start the program. This allows you to get the chapter leadership on board without rushing to organize and launch your program at the beginning of the year. Having an idea of what you want to accomplish and how you want to go about it also makes it more likely you will achieve the program goals.

At some point while reading this book, you may start to wonder just how much time it will take to get this program off the ground. The answer is maybe not as much time as you think. The purpose of the book is to give you a process to use to start your mentorship program and an idea of what to do as you move through that process.

The idea to start a mentorship program may come from the annual strategic planning process for your chapter leadership team, and they may take an entire year to decide how they want to proceed. It is also possible to design and start your program within a month so you keep the momentum and excitement generated when the idea was first proposed.

It's not important how long it takes to start your mentorship program. What is important is the process you follow at the beginning that gives your mentorship program the best chance of success. After the first year, it will be clear what is working and what needs to change. Your program will take shape as you make improvements each year.

Our advice is to have someone start the program who truly believes in the mentorship process. If a current member or one of the chapter leadership team is interested, ask them to lead the program the first year, give them this book, and watch it grow.

An Overview of the Process

We created this book as a guide for what to include in your first mentorship program. We hope a play-by-play description of our processes and pitfalls will help you get to the fun parts faster and minimize the challenges you encounter along the way. Here is a list of the steps to set up and run your mentorship program:

Planning – set the program goals; select your leader and committee members; determine the program details and establish your budget.

Marketing – create your marketing plan; select how you want to promote it; launch your mentorship program.

Selection – process applications from prospective participants; select and prepare both the mentors and the mentees; conduct a speed mentoring session to pair your mentors and mentees.

Training – orient your participants to the theoretical framework of the mentorship program; get the mentor-mentee pairs started in their relationship.

Facilitate – conduct monthly group meetings for both mentors and mentees; offer suggestions for group presentations to supporting the work of the mentor-mentee pairs.

Program Completion – use a brainstorming session with each group to find out what worked, what didn't work, and collect ideas for next year; give participants a chance to celebrate their work at the end of the program; provide chapter recognition for participants and a successful program.

Debrief – conduct a meeting of the mentorship committee to review results, suggestions, and plan for next year.

Resources Included

In the resource download area are documents and Microsoft PowerPoint® presentations we developed for use in our program. To help illustrate certain topics, links to a number of background articles detailing topics covered in the monthly meetings are also provided.

Chapter 2
HOW TO BEGIN

This chapter guides you through the start of your mentorship program. It provides guidelines on getting buy-in from the chapter leadership. It helps you set the program goals and choose a leader. Last, it walks you through creating your program plan and budget.

Knowing why you want to establish a mentoring program for your chapter will set the tone for the entire program. In turn, knowing "why" will help with the "how," such as selecting the program leader and determining the budget your first year. It will also help with the "what," such as the topics and speakers for the monthly program meetings.

Tie It to the Mission

The process of creating your mentorship program starts with the chapter leadership or board of directors. They are the group who will decide to start a new chapter program or initiative. You need their buy-in first before you can start the mentorship program.

In most chapters, the focus of the leadership and the volunteers is on fulfilling the mission and/or adding value for the members. One of the most important reasons for starting a new program is to increase the benefit for members to join or continue their membership with the chapter.

Every chapter has their own vision for how to achieve their mission. Here are some examples of chapter mission statements:

- To be a premier resource for our members while advancing our profession.
- To serve our professional members by providing comprehensive training, information, and resources to our members; to advance the Human Resource profession by supporting our community while ensuring HR is an essential and effective partner in developing and executing organizational strategy.
- To inspire and empower members to build organizational value through people.

Every year, your board of directors reviews and updates their strategic plan. Then they generate a list of the strategic goals they believe will assist them in achieving the chapter mission, and decide which activities are most likely to help them achieve the strategic goals. One of these goals may be to support the professional development of their members.

How your chapter board of directors learned about the value of mentorship could happen many different ways. Perhaps someone on the board of directors had experience with a formal mentoring program. Maybe a chapter member heard about a successful mentorship program in another chapter or from a friend at a conference.

Once the decision is made to begin a mentorship program, the board must also set goals for the program. These goals should link directly to the board's strategic plan for that year. For example, the goals for our mentorship program in the first year were:

- Create a developmental partnership through which mentors share their knowledge, skills, information, and perspective to foster the professional growth of their mentee.
- Support the chapter's objective of furthering the ongoing enhancement of a dynamic, diverse membership and, as a result, the HR profession through learning and networking.
- Give senior-level HR professionals an opportunity to "give back" to our members and our profession through a one-of-a-kind opportunity for collaboration, goal achievement, and problem solving.

The involvement of the board of directors in the decision to start a mentorship program and determine the program goals is critical. However, their influence extends far beyond that.

Having the board of directors committed to the new mentorship program also helps with word of mouth advertising when the program begins. They are visible to members as the chapter leadership. When they speak positively about the new program, it increases the interest of senior level HR professionals in participating as mentors. This in turn increases the chances of success for your mentorship program.

To set your program goals, start a discussion among the chapter leadership or board of directors. A logical place to begin is thinking about what the chapter hopes to gain by supporting this process. Agreement on the goals for the program is critical for the problem solving needed during your first year. These goals and objectives also provide a measurement tool for the program results.

We suggest that even in the beginning, your intent should be that the mentorship program benefits both early career and senior HR professional chapter members. Due to the differences in their professional experience, each group has different developmental needs.

Early career professionals benefit greatly from having a mentor to guide them. Senior HR professionals enjoy the chance to help someone with less HR experience advance in their career. By giving your more experienced chapter members the chance to share their knowledge, you will accomplish another goal: actively engaging some of your senior HR professionals who are chapter members. Even from the beginning, you will probably notice that the mentors who volunteer each year in the mentorship program may not attend chapter meetings but they maintain their chapter membership.

Choose Your Program Leader

Another reason the board is so deeply involved in starting the mentorship program is that they choose the first mentorship program leader. The choice of a mentorship program leader is one of the most important decisions in starting your mentorship program and is critical to the program's success. The leader selected may be a board member or a chapter member who is championing the start of the program.

In making this decision, the chapter leadership should look for someone with the characteristics of a good leader. They may want to keep the following leadership attributes in mind when making this decision:

Passion for Mentoring – Whatever their current involvement within the chapter, a necessary qualification for the mentorship program leader is a willingness to invest the necessary time and energy in starting the program. For this reason, the leader must be passionate about the value of mentoring, as well as the value of the program for the chapter and its members. They must be a champion for the mentorship program from the beginning. Their passion and commitment to the mentorship program is a big factor in the success of the program.

Personal Network – A large part of this role requires the ability to establish rapport easily. Look for someone well connected within your chapter.

Enthusiasm – There's a lot of work involved in beginning a new mentorship program. The board of directors should look for someone excited about starting the program. Enthusiasm for getting the program off the ground will help the leader stay positive during the process.

Established Professional – Being an established HR professional is important for this position. It gives your leader buy-in with the chapter membership and helps them effectively recruit the mentorship committee members and mentors. Also important is that the mentorship program leader is knowledgeable enough to lead the mentorship committee in selecting the topics for the monthly meetings.

Effective Meeting Leader –Select a leader who is comfortable leading meetings and driving the establishment of the mentorship program. It helps if the person is someone to whom others naturally look to run meetings.

When the chapter leadership has determined the knowledge, skills, and abilities most important for the mentorship program leader, they need to write and approve a job description for the role. Then the position needs to be advertised everywhere you can think of: the chapter newsletter, emails, and website, as well as the chapter LinkedIn® group and/or Facebook® page.

Using all these locations will get the word out about the new program. If two or more people apply to be the program leader, select the volunteer you believe is best qualified to lead. A sample job description is below.

Mentorship Program Leader Job Description

Qualifications

As mentorship program leader, you are outgoing, with skill in personal networking and starting new programs. You are experienced at leading others and running meetings. You are a good communicator and have a strong desire to provide career development opportunities for other HR professionals. Qualifications for the mentorship program leader include:

- Active chapter member
- Minimum five years HR experience; this can be a combination of HR management, generalist, consultant, or a specialist role (i.e., benefits, compensation, recruitment, etc.)
- Knowledgeable about current HR practices
- Skilled in preparing and managing budgets
- Experienced leader; demonstrated familiarity in planning and organizing the work of others, and in delegating and managing deadlines
- Willing to make a 12-month commitment to the mentorship program, program committee, and mentorship participants

---

Mentorship Program Leader Role

You will plan, organize, and direct other committee members throughout the entire mentorship program. You will lead the committee members, mentors, and mentees participating in the mentorship program. You have the above qualifications and are capable of carrying out the following responsibilities:

- Write the mentorship committee job descriptions
- Recruit and select the mentorship committee
- Work with the chapter board of directors and mentorship committee to decide the program details, budget, and marketing plan
- Schedule mentorship program meetings, decide program content and speaker schedule, and conduct committee and mentorship program meetings
- Communicate with mentorship program participants regarding acceptance and expectations for participation
- Schedule and conduct a training session for participants
- Facilitate ongoing mentorship program activities
- Evaluate participant feedback and progress reports for early signs of closure with mentor-mentee pairs
- Lead brainstorming sessions and all program-end activities
- Plan, prepare, and conduct a chapter recognition event

Note: This sample job description is included in Appendix A: Goal Setting and Planning.

Select the Mentorship Committee

Selecting the mentorship committee members will take less time and effort than finding the mentorship program leader. In fact, if the chapter leadership decides on a small program the first year, the program leader may decide to run the mentorship program without the support of a committee.

It's completely possible for one person to set up and run a mentorship program with only two to five mentor-mentee pairs. With more than five mentor-mentee pairs, there is plenty of work for one or more program committee volunteers in addition to the mentorship program leader. If you decide to start with more than five mentor-mentee pairs, the support of a mentorship committee will give the program the best chance for success. The number of volunteers you decide to recruit is up to the mentorship program leader.

If you choose to recruit a mentorship committee, the mentorship program leader must write a job description for the mentorship committee positions so people know the expectations before they volunteer. Chapter members who volunteered to lead the program and weren't selected may want to be part of the mentorship committee. Another possibility is your new program leader may know chapter members interested in helping to start the mentorship program. In either situation, there would be no need to advertise for mentorship committee volunteers.

However, if no volunteers are readily available, the mentorship program leader can recruit volunteers for the mentorship committee. Once the mentorship committee members are selected, they will decide the rest of the details about the first year's mentorship program. A sample mentorship committee member job description is below.

Mentorship Committee Member Job Description

Qualifications

As a mentorship committee member, you are a team player with attention to detail and enthusiastic about working with others. You are a strong communicator with a desire to provide career development opportunities for other HR professionals. Qualifications for the mentorship committee member include:

- Active chapter member
- Minimum of five years of HR experience; this can be a combination of HR management, generalist, consultant, or a specialist role (i.e., benefits, compensation, recruitment, etc.)
- Knowledgeable about current HR practices
- Willing to make a 12-month commitment to the mentorship program, program committee and mentorship participants
- Readily available by phone and/or email throughout the mentorship program

Mentorship Committee Role

You will plan, organize, and assist other committee members to facilitate professional growth for the mentorship program participants. You can demonstrate that you have the right qualifications and are capable of carrying out the following responsibilities:

- Work with other committee members to develop a marketing plan for the mentorship program
- Assist the mentorship program leader and other mentorship committee members with planning and preparing the mentorship program activities
- Participate in the participant selection process for both mentors and mentees; conduct interviews and review the results of mentor and mentee interviews
- Participate in mentoring program activities and discussions and in tracking program progress
- Attend meetings and provide follow-up assistance for committee members and/or program leader
- Assist in planning and preparing the chapter recognition event at the end of the program

Note: This sample job description is included in Appendix A: Goal Setting and Planning

---

Decide the Details

Once selected, the first job of the mentorship committee is to plan all the details related to the mentorship program. Some of these details are the number of mentor-mentee pairs to recruit, the program timeframe, number of meetings, meeting location(s), meeting schedule, and meeting topics. The committee also decides who will be responsible for each detail related to setting up and running the mentorship program.

Here is a list of some of the decisions the mentorship committee must make:

Program Detail	Decision
Program length	At least 6 months; up to 12 months
Length of program phases	Time for each phase: applications, interviews, pre-meetings, speed mentoring, training session
Program size	Number of mentor-mentee pairs
Applicant requirements	Mentor and mentee job descriptions
Application requirements	Résumé, application letter, and individual participation goals
Interviews	Write interview questions for both mentor and mentee applicants and conduct interviews
Decision matrix for program acceptance	Determine success factors for both mentors and mentees
Meeting logistics	Meeting types, frequency, location, cost, topics, presenters, refreshments, etc.
Budget	Determine the cost of the meeting locations(s), refreshments, gifts and materials, subject to Board approval

Program Length

During the planning process, the mentorship committee should carefully consider other chapter activities and choose the program length they believe will best achieve the goals of the participants and the chapter. We recommend your mentorship program be at least 9 - 10 months long.

One reason we recommend a program that's nine or more months in length is that it takes mentees at least six months to complete their developmental goals. A longer program gives them a better chance of achieving their goals. It also gives the mentorship committee the chance to make course corrections as your mentorship program evolves the first year.

Another factor to consider when determining your program length is that HRCI allows up to five recertification credits per year for volunteering as a mentor in the mentorship program.

This book describes how to set up a 12-month mentorship program. If you decide to have a 12-month program, the additional work for a longer program isn't burdensome, and your mentors will appreciate that they can claim all five HRCI recertification credits each year.

Program Timing

When planning your program, the committee must also consider what time of year to begin the process. The chart below is our suggestion for how to set up a 12-month, calendar-year program.

Note: Even though it's called a calendar-year program, the planning and recruiting for the program starts before January of the calendar year. In other words, the planning and application process for your 2016 mentorship program would begin in November of 2015.

We tried beginning our program at times other than January. We saw the best results with recruiting mentors and mentees by changing our mentor application period to the beginning of January. Starting early in the calendar year allows you to end your program in late November or December as the calendar year is winding down and before the holiday season gets underway. It also gives your mentees plenty of time to accomplish their career goals for the program.

Even if you decide to begin your program at a different time of year, we suggest you keep the interim program milestones as suggested in the timeline below. Refer to the months and weeks listed in the Time Frame column to help you decide your program schedule. You may also notice that with either a calendar year program or a mid-year program, the end of one mentorship program always overlaps with marketing the next year's program.

Time Frame	Calendar Month	Description
Month 1	November	Begin mentorship program marketing
Month 2	December	Mentor applications and interviews

Time Frame	Calendar Month	Description
Month 3, Week 1	January	Mentor selection and pre-meeting
Month 3, Weeks 2 - 3	January	Mentee applications, interviews, and selection
Month 3, Week 4	January	Mentees' pre-meeting
Month 4, Week 3	February	Speed mentoring
Month 5, Week 1	March	Training session
Months 5 – 12	March - October	Monthly program meetings
Month 13	November	Wrap up current program, recognize participants, and evaluate completed program; begin marketing for next mentorship program

Application Process Timing

The application period for your mentors should begin at least three weeks before the mentors' pre-meeting at the end of January. You may even want to start accepting mentor applications before the holiday season begins in December. This makes the mentor application period long, but the advantage of starting early is it gives you plenty of time to market your new program.

More marketing time is especially important the first year, because it allows the word-of-mouth campaign to reach more people. It also eliminates the time pressure on the mentorship committee if they choose to wait until January to market the mentorship program.

Our mentorship program always ends in November, immediately before the marketing of the next year's mentorship program begins. The challenge is the mentorship committee must start planning for the next year before the current mentorship program ends in November.

Each year in your November chapter meeting, you can provide special recognition to the mentorship program participants for their efforts. At the same meeting, we suggest you announce that the application period for the next year's mentorship program is officially open. That way, your will benefit from the positive publicity around the conclusion of the mentorship program to help with recruiting for the following year's program.

Meeting Schedule

This section discusses planning and scheduling the different types of group meetings in the mentorship program.

Introductory or Pre-Meetings

We recommend you hold two introductory or pre-meetings, one for the mentors and one for the mentees. Schedule your pre-meetings to be held shortly after you send the acceptance messages to each group of mentorship program participants. It's true that there's already plenty to do at this point in your first mentorship program without adding two more meetings to the schedule. However, including these two introductory meetings in the schedule will make your start-up process easier and save you time later.

Here's why: we noticed during the first few years of our mentorship program that our applicants all asked the same questions about the mentorship program. This was especially true for our prospective mentees.

Then one year we tried holding a very informal meeting for chapter members interested in becoming a mentee. There wasn't much advertising, just a few sentences on the chapter website. The agenda was simple: answer questions about the mentorship program and give prospective mentees a chance to meet one another.

Even in that first pre-meeting we noticed relationships forming that promised a more cohesive mentee group than any previous year. Based on that experience, we immediately scheduled a pre-meeting for the mentors, with even more positive results. Mentors from the previous year were there to share stories with newcomers about being a mentor, and all of them had the common bond of being senior HR professionals.

Later, the explanation for the success of the pre-meetings became clear. Mentorship participants who attend the pre-meeting get an earlier start on developing the network that is so beneficial to mentorship program participants. That's why we recommend you schedule pre-meetings for both mentors and mentees as part of your mentorship program.

During the mentors' pre-meeting you can explain the mentors' role in the mentee application process. If you use a formal application process in your mentorship program, it adds work for the mentorship committee. To provide them with some help, ask your mentors at the mentors' pre-meeting for assistance in interviewing the prospective mentees.

Because they are involved in interviewing the prospective mentees, the mentors' pre-meeting is scheduled for right before the mentee interviews begin. The mentees' pre-meeting is always immediately after they are selected for the program.

One thing that is the same for the mentors and mentees: both pre-meetings are scheduled in the evening on the same day as the monthly program meetings. This sets everyone's expectation from the beginning that mentorship program meetings are on the same day every month.

Speed Mentoring Meeting

Although there is an entire chapter later in this book about speed mentoring, it's important to note here that planning is the most important factor for success in the speed mentoring meeting.

Communication with all the mentorship program participants about how the process works is the second most important factor for success.

Both of these factors are interrelated. Since "speed" is an integral part of the process, the speed mentoring session needs careful planning to keep the momentum going throughout the entire meeting.

Due to the need for speed, each participant must understand his or her role in every step of the process. Once all their questions are answered and they understand what to do, everyone can "go with the flow" and have a good time getting to know each other.

The Speed Mentoring chapter contains a very detailed process for planning and conducting the speed mentoring meeting.

Training Session

After the mentorship participants are selected and the mentor-mentee pairs assigned, we recommend a training session to orient all the participants to the mentorship program. The training session serves as the official beginning of the mentorship program, and ensures that the mentor-mentee relationships begin with the necessary knowledge and tools for success.

When planning your program meetings, allow two to three hours for the training session. For the first several years, our training session lasted four hours, and feedback from participants told us four hours was too long. Our training session is now three hours on a Saturday morning.

Since the training session is scheduled about two weeks after the speed mentoring session, we recommend that two different mentorship committee members take responsibility for planning each of these sessions. Each committee member can then focus each on their respective responsibilities: one for planning and executing the speed mentoring session, and the other for planning and executing the training session.

The training session might seem like the most complex part of the entire mentorship program. There are a large number of details and logistical challenges to oversee, such as handouts, AV requirements, and refreshments, that are different from all the other mentorship program meetings. More details of planning and conducting your training session are covered in *Chapter 5: Training*.

Monthly Meetings: Mentor, Mentee, and Combined Group

After the training session, we recommend the mentors and mentees meet regularly each month. We've tried meeting as often as every three weeks and as infrequently as every six weeks.

Everyone's conclusion was that monthly group meetings are best.

To keep the schedule as consistent as possible, try to schedule the mentorship program meetings on the same night of the same week each month.

After the training session, schedule the first meeting as a combined group, with the mentors and mentees together. Then begin a cycle for each group to meet in their separate groups every other month.

It works well to schedule the combined mentee and mentor group meetings in the odd calendar months (March, May, July, and September).

Then in the even calendar months (April, June, August, October), schedule the mentees-only group meetings and the mentors-only group meetings on consecutive nights.

Coordinating Group Meetings – Schedule your first combined group meeting to be held about two weeks after the training session. That seems to be the right interval to hold the first monthly meeting of the mentorship program. It reinforces the expectation that there will be meetings at regular intervals for the remainder of the program.

If the first group meeting is scheduled less than two weeks after the training session, the participants complain about too many meetings. If you wait longer than two weeks for the first group meeting, the participants have a tendency to forget their commitment to the program.

Deciding when and how often to schedule the group meetings during the mentorship program is an art, not a science.

Too frequent, and the participants may decide the program is too much work. If that happens, attendance at the group meetings will go down, or participants will drop out of the program.

If the meetings are too infrequent, the participants will feel disconnected from the group, which is another cause for low meeting attendance or attrition in the group.

Consistency is very important in setting the schedule for the mentorship program meetings. It works especially well when the meetings are scheduled on the same night each month, and the meeting schedule for the entire program is published in advance.

There are several advantages to this approach:

Mentorship program participants can (and do!) add the group meetings to their calendars at the beginning of the program for the entire year, increasing the likelihood they will attend the meetings.

Knowing in advance the number and frequency of the required meetings ensures they are aware of the required program commitments.

It also helps them when scheduling all their other activities.

By knowing in advance which nights they are already committed, it motivates them to schedule other events on different nights and helps avoid attendance issues at the monthly program meetings.

It is even important to consider the week of the month and the nights of the week you schedule your mentorship program meetings. We've tried every week of the month and every weeknight when scheduling our mentorship program group meetings. We even tried holding group meetings on Saturdays. We were promptly discouraged from that practice by a significant drop in attendance. Mentorship participants were quick to point out they consider their weekends to be family and personal time, not professional time.

Keeping in mind that your participants have lives outside the mentorship program, you might try asking them which nights they have other commitments.

Many organizations schedule events on Wednesday and Thursday nights. Tuesdays are next in popularity. Mondays and Fridays are the least popular nights for scheduling professional, sports, or scholastic events.

After a lot of experimentation, we suggest you schedule the mentee group meetings on Monday evenings, with the mentor and combined group meetings on Tuesdays.

To avoid scheduling the mentee meetings on national holidays that are often on Monday, schedule your monthly group meetings the second week of the month. Fortunately, national holidays rarely occur on the second Monday of the month, making this schedule very workable.

To keep the combined versus individual group meetings consistent:

- Schedule your combined group meetings on the second Tuesday in the *odd* calendar months (March, May, July, September, and November).
- Schedule the separate mentor and mentee group meetings on the second Monday and Tuesday of the *even* calendar months (April, June, August, and October).

Scheduling the mentor-only group meeting the day after the mentee-only group meeting is intentional. It allows the mentors a chance to hear about the mentee-only meeting the night before. You can also make sure the mentors are informed about any pertinent discussions from the mentee-only meeting in case they need the information for discussions with their mentee that month.

Using this arrangement will also add consistency to your mentors' schedules. The mentors are volunteering their time for the professional development of the mentees. In return, we recommend scheduling all their mentorship program meetings on the second Tuesday of each month as both a courtesy and an acknowledgement of their contribution.

Deciding Meeting Time and Length – Of equal importance to which night of the week meetings are scheduled is the starting and ending time for your monthly meetings. We suggest you schedule your mentorship program meetings after regular work hours.

Your chapter members may find that the unpredictability of traffic makes a difference in how long it takes them to get to the meeting location. If the meetings begin too early, a majority of the participants arrive after the meeting starts. Starting too late decreases the number of program participants and causes problems with attendance.

After several years of experimentation, we settled on a start time of 6 pm. Some people still have to leave work early to arrive on time for the meetings, but starting later than

6 pm practically guarantees there will be those who will not volunteer for the mentorship program due to family commitments.

Another consideration is the length of the group meetings. Starting the meetings at 6 pm automatically adds limitations since the meetings are on a work night. People need to get home at a reasonable hour to connect with their family, prepare for the following workday, and have a little time to relax before bedtime.

Some of your mentorship program participants may use public transportation. This decreases their options for evening travel. Other participants may live up to an hour away from the meeting location. For these reasons, a meeting length of over two hours just isn't practical. Another consideration is that meetings over two hours must have break time built into the agenda, making the meetings even longer, and adding constraints to the meeting content.

On the other hand, scheduling your meetings for less than two hours also creates problems. Mentorship program participants have trouble seeing the value of spending the time to get to a meeting scheduled for 90 minutes, and then turning right around and going home. A two-hour meeting seems to have higher value for them, and attendance at the longer meetings is consistently higher. In addition, if a meeting scheduled for 90 minutes runs longer than expected, you will probably hear complaints and rumblings in the group about the time commitment required for the mentorship program.

Another factor to consider is your guest speakers. They benefit from having an hour or more to speak with time remaining for questions. A two-hour meeting also allows plenty of time for small group discussions during the presentation. All group activities, especially in smaller groups, are highly prized by our mentorship program participants.

Occasionally, in a two-hour meeting with topics that invite discussion, you may have to remind the group that it's time to leave! And if a group meeting runs shorter than the full two hours, no one ever complains if they get the chance to leave before 8 pm.

For all these reasons, we recommend scheduling your mentorship program meetings for two hours, from 6 pm to 8 pm.

Monthly Meeting Attendance – If participants are going to reap the benefits of the mentorship program, it is critical to require and track attendance at the monthly group meetings. One of the benefits most prized by your mentorship program participants will be the relationships they form during the program. It's difficult for someone to feel connected to the group and form strong relationships if they don't attend group meetings. The importance of everyone being at all the group meetings can't be over-emphasized.

It's important for you to say early and often that attendance at group meetings is required for all mentorship program participants. State from the beginning in every way you can find that meeting attendance is mandatory. This is why we suggest you set the program meeting dates before the program begins. We also recommend that you provide chapter members with a copy of the schedule as soon as they apply.

If you make attendance at the program group meetings a requirement to be in the mentorship program, tracking attendance becomes critical. Some scheduling conflicts are unavoidable, and life happens. This is why you need to follow up each time someone misses a group meeting. It demonstrates to your mentorship participants that the mentorship committee is serious about requiring attendance.

If the mentorship committee doesn't pay attention to attendance, the program participants won't either. At that point, the value they place on the mentorship program decreases with every missed meeting. Missing a group meeting is often an early warning sign that a participant is not getting value from the mentorship program, or the relationship with their mentor or mentee is not working.

Part of the planning process is to decide which mentorship committee member will track attendance and follow up with anyone who misses a scheduled meeting. We strongly suggest that the mentorship committee decide during the planning process which individual will follow up, and how soon, with participants who miss a group meeting. It is also critical to make sure the follow-up message is one of concern, not enforcement of the mentorship program "rules."

Individual Mentor-Mentee Meetings

A requirement of your mentorship program should be that each mentor-mentee pair meets at regular intervals during the program. The purpose of these individual meetings is to review and discuss the mentee's progress toward their goals for the mentorship program. These meetings are a critical piece in developing the one-to-one mentoring relationship between each mentor and their mentee.

Program evaluations show that mentees who meet with their mentor every month are more likely to achieve their developmental goals for the mentorship program, and mentor-mentee pairs who meet less often don't achieve the same results. Feedback from successful mentor-mentee pairs has demonstrated that they believe the monthly meetings were crucial to meeting the mentee's development goals.

To give everyone the best chance of success, tell all your mentorship program applicants that the expectation for the program is they will meet with their mentor or mentee at least once per month. Setting this expectation in advance allows potential applicants to weigh their commitment to the mentoring program before they apply. If someone isn't committed to the amount of work it takes to have a successful partnership with their mentor or mentee, they usually decide not to apply to the program.

The reverse is also true. Knowing the requirement of individual monthly meetings in advance, if someone applies to the mentorship program and is accepted, it is with the knowledge that they need to take their commitment to meet once per month with their mentor or mentee seriously.

You can definitely leave it up to the mentor-mentee pairs to decide where and when to meet. It does help if they are not geographically distant. Before the mentors and mentees mark their ballots at the speed mentoring session, you may want to suggest that they consider teaming up with someone who lives or works nearby their home or place of work.

Sometimes mentors or mentees choose each other knowing the logistics of meeting every month will prove daunting. In those cases, alert them to the increased difficulty and take a watchful approach. For about half of the geographically distant mentor-mentee pairs, it will probably become too difficult to meet every month and they may drop out before the end of the program. The other half find a way to make it work to meet every month, and they stay in the program through the end.

Some mentor-mentee pairs decide at the beginning of the mentorship program that they will meet more frequently than once a month. Others make this decision in response to an issue the mentee is dealing with at work, and then revert to monthly meetings once the crisis is resolved. The additional time commitment of meeting more than once a month can be difficult, especially for the mentors.

When a mentor tells you they are meeting more than once per month with their mentee, ask if they need additional resources or support from the mentorship committee. If helps to also ask them to communicate with you as soon as possible if the increased commitment is not sustainable. Then stay alert to signs of burnout on the part of the mentor.

In about half of these instances, the mentor may find it too exhausting to incorporate additional meetings with their mentee into their professional and family commitments, with the result that the mentor or both the mentor and the mentee quit the program early. This happens in spite of their best intentions in stepping up their meeting schedule. However, the decision to meet more frequently can also benefit mentor-mentee pairs; about half of the mentor-mentee pairs who choose to meet more than once a month experience a real benefit from these additional meetings.

Mentor-Mentee Progress Forms – With the requirement that the mentor-mentee pairs meet monthly, it becomes important to have a way to track these meetings. Since the mentor-mentee pairs have complete control over where and when they met, we suggest using a progress form to help with follow-up on this requirement.

Send the progress form to all the mentorship program participants at the beginning of the program to use each month. At minimum, ask them to include the date, time, and length of each monthly meeting, along with at least one sentence about what was discussed. Returning the form each month with these details then demonstrates they have fulfilled the requirement to meet with their mentor or mentee.

Note: See Appendix F: Monthly Program Meetings *for a progress form example. It is also available in the Resources Download area.*

During the planning phase, it's important for the mentorship committee to decide who will distribute and collect the monthly progress forms. It usually works well to have the mentorship committee member in charge of tracking attendance at the monthly group meeting to be in charge of the mentor-mentee progress forms.

Remember, notify your mentorship program participants at the beginning of the program about these requirements and processes. We've found that setting the expectations early and consistently following up when participants miss a meeting prevents small problems from developing into big ones.

Mentor Sub-Group "Quad" Meetings

A frequent comment from our mentors the first few years of our mentorship program was that although they really liked contributing to the career development of a less-experienced HR person, they wanted more value for themselves and their own career. In other words, getting recertification credit is nice but mentors also want something a little more tangible in return for their participation in the mentorship program.

One year during the program-end brainstorming session, a mentor asked us to find a way for the mentors to connect with each other. She pointed out that the mentor group meetings scheduled every other month weren't sufficient to establish that kind of connection. As she put it, "We all know it takes a village to raise a mentee. What we really need is a way for the mentors to feel more like a village."

The following year during the pre-meeting, we created small groups of four mentors, based on their geographic proximity, and asked these mentor "sub-groups" to try meeting for lunch once a month to network. Since there were four mentors in each sub-group, they quickly named themselves mentor "quads."

One year was all it took for the mentors to decide these sub-groups should be a permanent part of any mentorship program. Mentors form stronger relationships with each other during their "quad" meetings. It helps them act more like a village and work together to support their mentees more successfully. The sub-groups are self-sustaining, so there is no need to track whether the mentors meet each month. The mentors find so much value in these meetings that they make sure their sub-group meetings are scheduled and attended by everyone.

Forming these smaller groups of mentors works best if your mentorship program has eight or more mentors. If you decide to make it a permanent part of your mentorship program, each year you will see and hear the "villageness" effect begin as soon as the mentor sub-groups meet for the first time.

An interesting effect: you would think because the mentor sub-groups were so successful, the mentees deserve to reap the same benefit. We tried it, but the mentees saw it as another chore for them in the mentorship program. None of the mentee sub-groups met more than three or four times during the entire year of the mentorship program. After that, we decided there wasn't enough value for the mentees and eliminated it as part of their participation in the mentorship program.

Final Program Meeting

We mention the final program meeting in the planning phase in case you choose to follow our example and make the last meeting more of a celebration. If you do, it helps to plan this meeting well in advance due to the differences in meeting agenda and refreshments provided.

Because the last program meeting is a combined group meeting, two mentorship program participants (a mentor and a mentee) will have signed up to provide snacks and non-alcoholic beverages for the entire group at the final program meeting.

The difference at the last program meeting is that the chapter may want to provide additional refreshments such as cake, champagne, or other additions to help with the celebration. More details about planning and conducting the final mentorship program meeting are discussed in detail in *Chapter 8: Program Completion.*

Social Events: Yes or No?

We have gone back and forth on the value of planning social functions for the mentorship program participants. Our logic is if it is a social function, then attendance should be voluntary.

Another thing to consider is that any social functions are usually in addition to the monthly mentorship meetings. They may be on weekends, and occasionally family and partners are invited. The interest in weekend events, and inviting family and/or partners, has varied considerably from year to year among our mentorship participants.

For these and other reasons, we recommend that your mentorship committee not be involved in planning social events. If the mentorship program participants want to schedule a social event, encourage them to talk with the other participants to determine interest and make their decision based on the feedback they receive.

Meeting Logistics

A key factor to the success of your mentorship program is managing the meeting logistics. Handling these details is where the committee members make a big difference in the success of your mentorship program.

Location, Location, Location

We could write an entire book just on finding locations to hold your mentorship program meetings. Budgetary constraints kept us from being able to pay for our meeting location. During the first three years of our mentorship program, we fought a constant battle to find a location for the meeting each month.

Unfortunately, most public places such as libraries and municipal offices don't accept standing reservations. They also don't allow meeting space reservations more than two weeks in advance.

Finding a place to meet and communicating that location to the program participants each month became a constant frustration for the mentorship committee. In addition, we couldn't confirm every participant received that month's meeting details. The participants who did receive it didn't always RSVP to the meetings. This cycle repeated itself every month during the program.

Without a consistent place to hold the program meetings, most of your time managing the mentorship program will revolve around these issues. It affects every aspect of your program. With the committee spending so much time finding and communicating the meeting location, there will be no time left to work on improving your group meetings.

You also can't hold people responsible for their attendance if they didn't get the meeting announcement. Several times, we found a place to meet just a few days before the scheduled date. That led to late arrivals, and to some people just not coming because they couldn't find the building. Most important, and most detrimental, nearly all our communications with the program participants was related the meeting location details, and not about the value of their participation in the program.

The importance of arranging your monthly meeting locations before the program starts is probably very clear by now. Take the time during the planning phase to find and reserve meeting space for all the mentorship program meetings so you have more time once the program is underway to focus on other details.

Knowing the meeting locations in advance is also one of the surest ways to guarantee attendance at the group meetings. When program participants add the meetings to their calendars, the location will always be the same. They soon learn how to find the meeting location and the length of time it takes to travel there.

We recommend you start your meeting planning processes by asking other chapter volunteers if they know of any free, available meeting space. Ask if they have a good working relationship with any local organizations that allow the use of their conference space during the evening at mid-week. You can also ask your mentorship program participants if anyone can volunteer space at their company headquarters for the monthly meetings.

Once you secure your meeting space, you may still have to scout for alternate locations several times during the program, but it will be a vast improvement over changing locations each month. In the months the meetings are in the "usual" location, your mentorship committee will notice how much extra time they have to spend on other aspects of the mentorship program. The time it takes to run the mentorship program overall will be significantly less, and you can use that time to find ways to add value to your mentorship program.

Planning Refreshments

It is important to plan how you want to handle refreshments for all the mentorship program meetings. Since the meetings are in the evening, most participants traveling directly from work won't have time to stop for food on their way to the meeting. Having some food and beverages available at the beginning of each meeting is both considerate and necessary.

Given that, try to strike a balance between the chapter providing food for the meetings and the mentorship participants providing the food themselves. There are several issues with the chapter providing the food for all the mentorship meetings:

Cost – The first issue with needing refreshments at every meeting is cost. Purchasing food is always more expensive than making it yourself. Even buying prepared food from a grocery store costs more, and food that is catered or delivered (pizza, for example) will have a delivery charge in addition to the increased expense.

If the chapter foots the bill for food at every mentorship program meeting, it adds substantially to the cost of starting your program. Even with the support of the chapter leadership team, it's still important to review the cost of the mentorship program and look for ways to save money. It's better to spend your mentorship program budget on expenses that only the chapter can provide. The mentorship program participants may have no problem providing food for the meetings, but they would expect the chapter to pay for other costs, such as meeting location fees.

Time – The second issue with refreshments provided by the chapter is the amount of time and energy it takes the mentorship committee to decide what to order, place the order, and make sure the delivery arrives on time with the correct food. Someone will need to arrive early for the food delivery. If your mentorship program meetings are in an office building, figuring out how to let the delivery person into the building after office hours and getting them access to the elevators adds another layer of complexity.

Paying at Delivery – Another concern is paying for the food at the time it's ordered or on delivery. Even if the mentorship committee member in charge of the refreshments is willing to use their own credit card, no one really wants to wait an entire year to be reimbursed for the cost of the mentorship program refreshments. Processing an expense report each month to ensure the member is reimbursed in a timely manner takes even more time for both the committee member and the chapter treasurer.

Food Preferences and Allergies – The last, but certainly not the least, issue to consider are the food preferences and allergies of the mentorship program participants. This is the most important reason why it makes sense for you not to provide refreshments for mentorship group meetings.

No matter how conscientious you are, it is almost impossible to provide food for 15 – 30 people and satisfy everyone's dietary needs. In the era of gluten-free, vegetarian, vegan, non-dairy, and other dietary preferences, it is incredibly difficult to find a place that provides food for every requirement.

Even if you find a place that works for everyone's dietary needs, it takes a great deal of care to decide on food that accommodates everyone's preferences. Then you have to factor in whether that place delivers. If not, a mentorship committee member is required to pick up and bring the food to the meeting. Sometimes the person ordering the food is not the same person who picks it up. They may have no way to know if the order is accurate or complete. Usually, anywhere that meet all your requirements and preferences will be very expensive.

Last, how will you decide what cuisine to choose or the number of questions that must be asked about the individual dishes in the order? Make the decision now for your mentorship committee to stay out of the food business. A nice balance is for the mentorship committee to provide refreshments only for the two mentorship program pre-meetings, the training session, and the final program meeting.

Refreshment Sign-up

We suggest you ask your mentorship program participants to provide the refreshments for the monthly group meetings. At the training session, ask the mentors and mentees to sign up to provide refreshments for one of the monthly group meetings.

With this method, the participants are responsible for asking about preferences and allergies among their group, and for bringing enough food and beverages for everyone at the meeting that month. Let them know there are no restrictions on what they choose to bring, or how they divide the responsibility. Sometimes one person can bring food and the other brings beverages. Sometimes they shop together, sometimes separately. Occasionally, one person has more time and shops for both and they split the cost. There are times when a participant brings a homemade dish, which everyone appreciates. Since your meetings will probably be in an office building or meeting space, there is usually some sort of kitchen on the premises for any required food assembly. We've never had a problem with electricity being available for slow cookers, etc.

One very positive outcome of signing up to bring refreshments is the participants get the opportunity to work with another mentee or mentor to plan and purchase the meeting refreshments. For the combined group meetings with both mentors and mentees, between two to four people work together to provide food for the entire group. In all the years of our mentorship program, no one has ever complained or refused to sign up and bring refreshments.

Meeting Topics

The monthly meeting topics for your mentorship program are limited only by your imagination. We recommend that your mentee-only group meetings be somewhat structured, with the goal of furthering the mentees' professional development.

At the combined mentor-mentee meetings, the meeting topics are broader and provide more depth. This gives the mentor-mentee pairs information to discuss in addition to the mentee's specific program goals in their monthly 1:1 scheduled meetings. A list of the meeting topics you might want to use in your mentee group, mentor group, and combined group meetings is below, with more detail provided in *Chapter 8, Monthly Program Meetings*.

Mentee Group Meetings

- Prior mentees: Q & A on their experience as a mentee
- Being a connector: networking for the 21st century
- Maximizing your LinkedIn profile
- Personal branding
- Case studies, facilitated by the mentorship program leader
- Current president: Q & A on being a chapter leader / chapter volunteer opportunities

Mentor Group Meetings

- Round robin check-ins / open mike
- Global HR
- Diversity and inclusion

Mentor and Mentee Combined Group Meetings

- Global HR
- Diversity and inclusion
- Case studies with role-playing by mentors
- Informational interview practice

Deciding in advance which topics to use for your group meetings is essential. The mentorship committee needs time to locate speakers on a specific topic or to prepare a presentation themselves. Starting the process sooner yields better results. Asking the speakers early on about reserving time on their calendars helps when confirming their availability. For all these reasons, choosing your meeting topics during the planning phase makes sense.

Meeting Details Worksheet

Below is a worksheet with details that apply to each type of mentorship program meeting. You can read more about each item in the section related to that meeting or event. This list will give you a starting point for planning the meetings in your mentorship program.

Meeting or Event	Frequency	Length	Need Facility or Room	Program Materials	AV Equipment	Refreshments	Gifts
Mentors pre-meeting	Once	2 hours	Yes	Yes	No	Chapter	No
Mentees pre-meeting	Once	2 hours	Yes	Yes	No	Chapter	No
Training session	Once	3 hours	Yes	Yes	Yes	Chapter	Yes
Combined group meetings	Every other month	2 hours	Yes	Yes	Depends	Participants	No

Meeting or Event	Frequency	Length	Need Facility or Room	Program Materials	AV Equipment	Refreshments	Gifts
Mentor group meetings	Every other month	2 hours	Yes	Yes	Depends	Participants	No
Mentee group meetings	Every other month	2 hours	Yes	Yes	Depends	Participants	No
Mentor quad meetings	Monthly	1 hour	No	No	No	Participants	No
Final program meeting	Program end	2 hours	Yes	Yes	No	Participants & chapter	Yes

The checklist below can be helpful when planning your meeting logistics.

Meeting Detail	Choices
Refreshments	Yes or no? Provided by chapter or participants? Food and beverage?
Group meetings	Monthly? More or less often? Track attendance? Follow up on missed meetings?
Meeting topics and presenters	Determine monthly meeting topics and arrange for presenters on each topic
Group meeting types	Separate group meetings? Combined? Alternate odd/even months?
Frequency of mentor-mentee individual meetings	Monthly? More or less often? Track progress?
Mentor small group meetings (quads)	How many per group? Geographic basis for group formation?
Meeting location	Free or paid? Geographical considerations? Local business or volunteer's employer? Availability for all program dates?

Note: *This checklist is included in* Appendix A: Goal Setting and Planning *and can be downloaded from the Resources Download area.*

Mentorship Program Budget

The last part of the planning phase is determining the budget for the mentorship program. Setting the budget for the first mentorship program should be the job of the mentorship committee, not the chapter leadership.

The mentorship committee should provide the board with a mentorship program budget for their approval, and make revisions if the first version is not approved. Chapters with tight budgets may decide not to spend chapter funds for the first year of the mentorship program. Doing this will take more ingenuity and planning by the mentorship committee to find sponsorship and no-cost ways to run the program, but it can be done.

Waiting until the first mentorship committee meeting to set the program budget allows you to tap into everyone's ideas. Their creativity can save you time and money, such as finding free meeting locations for the program meetings or arranging to have participants bring refreshments rather than having them catered.

In our case, the employer of one of the mentorship committee members underwrites all the printing costs for the mentorship program. It is always easier to find creative solutions as a committee rather than as an individual.

Meeting Locations

There are several main expense categories for the mentorship program budget. The first is the meeting venue cost. Meeting venues can be expensive, and the cost multiplies quickly when you have one or more meetings every month. Over time, we have found that saving money on venue costs is a great way to minimize your mentorship program budget. If you pay for meeting space each month, the chapter cost for the mentorship program will increase exponentially.

Unlike your monthly group meetings, the training session requires multimedia capability and it's not always possible to find a free meeting location with this requirement. You may not know when creating the mentorship budget if you need to rent a room for the training session. Include money in the budget each year for the training session venue, just in case. Then, when the chapter leadership approves the budget with that expense included, you won't have to go back and ask for more funds. It's also a pretty good bet that the chapter leadership won't mind if you don't spend the entire mentorship program budget each year.

Refreshments

Another expense to include in your budget is refreshments for the two mentorship program pre-meetings, the training session, and the party at the last program meeting.

While the refreshments don't need to be elaborate, you should account for those expenses in your budget. If your training session is on a Saturday morning, it helps if everyone is well fed and caffeinated during the meeting. The brunch provided at the training session is the largest budgetary expense for refreshments. Even with the expense of a cake for the wrap-up meeting at the end of the mentorship program, you will probably still spend more on the training brunch than on any mentorship program meeting.

We suggest that you plan for the mentorship committee to provide the utensils for every group meeting. During the planning phase, buy enough plates, cups, napkins, and eating utensils to last the entire mentorship program. Then you will have all the utensils needed for each meeting, and the participants will only need to provide food and drinks for the meetings.

Gifts

In the sample budget below, you'll notice that approximately half of the budgeted expenses are gifts for the mentorship program participants. Part of the money budgeted for gifts are for the training session. At the training session, each mentorship program participant receives a $5 gift card to use at a local coffee shop. They can use the cards any time, although the intent is to use them for their first mentor-mentee monthly meeting.

Why coffee cards? Not everyone drinks coffee, and many people prefer meeting somewhere other than a coffee shop. However, most of your mentorship program participants will understand the intent of the gift card and appreciate the gesture even if they choose to meet somewhere other than at a coffee shop. If your mentorship committee chooses to give a small gift to the participants to help them get acquainted, buying the gifts from a local landmark is a nice touch, and should be included in your budget.

It's also not necessary to buy everyone a gift at the end of your mentorship program. The chapter contributes to the development of the participants in many ways throughout a year-long program. You could make the argument that the experience of participating in the mentorship program is itself a gift from the chapter. More on the topic of gifts is included in *Chapter 8: Program Completion.*

Mentorship Program Budget			
Category	**Cost/Each**	**Number**	**Total Cost**
Participant Gifts			
Starbucks™ cards	$5.00	30	$150.00
Mentor gifts	$50.00	15	$750.00
Mentee gifts	$15.00	15	$225.00
Meetings			
Training brunch	$500.00	1	$500.00
Wrap-up meeting	$200.00	1	$200.00
Plates, napkins and utensils	$50.00	1	$50.00
Training room	$200.00	1	$200.00
Pre-meeting refreshments	$100.00	2	$200.00
TOTAL - Mentorship Budget			$2,275.00

Program Materials

Over the years, we've created a number of handouts and training materials (listed in the appendix) that are a part of our mentorship program training session and group meetings. Printing these materials can be expensive and should be included in the budget if you decide to use them.

You may decide to look for a sponsor to underwrite the expense of your printed materials. The sponsor can pay the cost of the printing, or do the printing in their office. This saves the mentorship committee time as well as eliminating an expense for the mentorship program. The money saved can be used for other mentorship program expenses.

Cutting Costs

A last word about budgeting: none of the expenses in the sample budget above are required for you to have a successful mentorship program.

If your chapter has a limited budget, there are many ways to save money.

For example, you don't have to give gifts to the participants at the end of the mentorship program. They are a nice touch, but not essential.

Holding the training session in the evening would eliminate a large expense for meeting refreshments.

Another alternative to the chapter bearing the expense of the mentorship program is to advertise for a sponsor for the entire mentorship. It is a great marketing tool for companies associated with your chapter.

If the choice is either spending the amount of money listed in the sample budget or not starting your mentorship program, we recommend finding ways to cut costs and start your mentorship program. The benefits of having a mentorship program for the chapter and the chapter members will definitely be worth the effort it takes to cut costs.

Mentorship Committee Authority

Before going further, it's important to state that there is no right way to set up and run a mentorship program. Some decisions that need to be made during the planning phase of starting your mentorship program are obvious. For example, if one of your mentorship committee members knows of a free location to hold the program meetings, it's worth using that location the first year to see if it meets all the requirements of the program.

A decision that may take a great deal of discussion is what night of the week to hold the mentorship program meetings. In that case, everyone will most likely have a preference, and choosing an evening that works for everyone may be a compromise.

With all the decisions that need to be made by the mentorship committee, it's critical that the chapter leadership concedes full authority for running the program to the mentorship committee as soon as the decision is made to start the program. Many, many decisions need to be made after that first choice to start a new program. If the chapter leadership insists on approving each decision, the committee's work and the mentorship program will come to a standstill.

In addition, many decisions related to starting this new program must be made on the spot. If the chapter leadership empowers the decision-making of the mentorship committee, the mentorship program is much more likely to be successful. Withholding the authority to make those decisions will ensure the mentorship program never gets past the talking stage.

We firmly believe that the success of our mentorship program comes from choosing the right leader for the program and then giving them freedom to run the program. Let your mentorship program leader know that the chapter leadership is always interested in hearing about the progress of the mentorship program but will not interfere with the day-to-day program details.

Summary

This chapter covers the process of starting your mentorship program, from the decision to start your program, though setting the program goals, recruiting and selecting a mentorship program leader and mentorship committee, and deciding the details of your program plan and budget.

Here are some of the factors mentioned that contribute to effective program planning:

- Well-defined program goals and objectives with support from the board of directors
- A program leader experienced and skilled in leadership, organization, and communication
- Enthusiastic committee members skilled at managing and scheduling meetings
- A detailed program plan and budget
- Full authority given to the mentorship committee to make decisions once the budget is approved
- Commitment from all program participants
- Well-planned meetings that are consistent and factor in scheduling issues of the participants

As you begin planning the details of your program, you can always refer back to the information provided in this chapter.

CHAPTER 3

MARKETING

When you've finished planning your mentorship program, it's time to put together your marketing plan. This chapter covers choosing your marketing approach and what to include in writing the content for your marketing campaign. It also contains detailed information on several different venues to advertise your program.

As you create your marketing plan, refer to the details of your mentorship program plan and the approved budget if needed. Your marketing plan should be based on those details, which will in turn help you achieve the goals for the program.

Building Your Marketing Plan

There is no best way to market and advertise your mentorship program. How you choose to promote it, especially the first year, will be as unique as your chapter.

The marketing techniques that work for a chapter with less than 100 members may not work for a larger chapter, and vice versa. There is no bad way to advertise and promote your mentorship program. All methods of communication serve to get the word out that the chapter is starting a new program.

In small chapters, the members may all know each other, so word-of-mouth may be the best technique to publicize the chapter's decision to start a mentorship program and promote it to participants. Some small chapters may have a phone tree; this would be a great method to advertise your mentorship program.

In larger chapters, especially those with more than 1,000 members, most of the members don't know each other. In those instances, review what works for other chapter programs when deciding how to promote your new mentorship program.

The mentorship committee should give themselves permission to try all the ideas they have the time, energy, and budget to implement. The way to measure success of an idea or marketing tactic is to compare the response rate for each one to all the other approaches you try. Some will be more effective than others. Find out what works, keep doing it, and add new ideas to the marketing plan for your mentorship program the following year. We've tried many approaches and messaging since starting our mentorship program and usually add at least one new idea each year.

For the first year, it's critical that the mentorship program leader sets the expectation with the mentorship committee members that all ideas are useful and everyone's marketing ideas have equal weight. Try using ideas that were successful for your other chapter programs. Some ideas for marketing your program may be unique to the mentorship committee members and the way they work together.

Crafting Your Message

The message is key to the success of your marketing plan.

For better or worse, everyone listens to marketing communications through the filter of "WIIFM" or "What's In It for Me?" To craft your marketing message, start by listing the benefits of the mentorship program for both mentors and mentees, because their reasons for participation are different.

Answering this question of WIIFM with a compelling reason to participate will increase the number of applicants for your mentorship program. Mentors may see this as their chance to help someone junior to them develop and move to the next step in their HR career. Mentees should see this program as their chance to learn HR best practices from a senior HR professional.

We also found that our marketing message must appeal to a higher level of benefit for the participant.

To illustrate, one year our marketing message for mentors emphasized the fact they could get HRCI recertification credit for participating in the mentorship program. That year, we had several mentors whose sole reason for volunteering was that they needed the HRCI credit. They were uninvolved in the program, did not attend most of the meetings, and several dropped out mid-program. The experience taught us that *HRCI recertification credit is not enough motivation for mentors to complete the requirements of our mentorship program.*

We learned another valuable lesson that year: because of the significant time investment required, it is important to emphasize the rigor of the program. We now tell everyone early and often just how much will be required of them to participate in the mentorship program.

It may seem as though emphasizing the program time requirements would discourage chapter members from participating in the program. We found just the opposite to be true. Knowing the program requirements in advance, the participants can make an informed choice and are more likely to comply with the requirements.

If participants apply with full knowledge of what the program entails, there is a much better chance of them being committed to fulfilling those requirements. We have found this leads to a higher percentage of participants finishing the entire program. Since we began emphasizing the time commitment to participate in the program, our participants have shown a higher level of satisfaction with the results of their investment of time and energy is higher.

An extra benefit of this marketing approach relates to the mentorship committee members. They will spend less time as enforcers of the program requirements, such as attendance at the monthly meetings, and more time helping the participants get the most value from their participation in the program.

For all these reasons, we suggest that the first year of your mentorship program you start with a small program whose participants are committed to dedicating the time and energy required.

An interesting side effect of the "full-disclosure" approach is that chapter members consider very carefully whether they have the time to devote to the program requirements. Several people have commented that they waited a year to apply to the mentorship program to be sure they had arranged their schedules to accommodate the required monthly meetings.

Marketing Content

For the first two or three years of our program, we asked participants to fill out a simple form on the chapter website requesting to become a mentor or mentee in the next mentorship program.

We changed this marketing strategy once we realized that for both mentees and mentors, a frequent outcome of participation in our mentorship program is a new job at a higher level, or one with more responsibility. Because of the very real possibility that participants may gain enough skill or expand their network sufficiently to change jobs during the mentorship program, it's a good idea to tell applicants to think of their mentorship program participation as a year-long job application.

With this approach, your application process needs to reflect the idea of the year-long job application. You will notice that the mentorship program description below reads like a job posting. It lists the position requirements for both mentors and mentees, including a detailed description of the time commitment to participate in our mentorship program.

Why An Application Process?

The information provided by the chapter members as part of their mentorship application is used multiple times throughout the program.

In addition, keeping the process similar to applying and interviewing for a job intentionally underscores the importance of the application process for your mentorship program participants, including their commitment to the mentorship program.

What you mean when you tell applicants to treat the mentorship program like a year-long job interview is universal knowledge for anyone who has ever applied for a job. It's one way to underscore the thoroughness, professionalism, and timeliness expected of your mentorship program participants.

As your mentorship program gains champions within the chapter over the years, you will find you have more applicants than spaces available. The mentorship program will be seen as a significant benefit of chapter membership. It's a valuable résumé addition for a participant to be chosen for the program. In our chapter, mentorship program participation has become similar to landing a coveted job.

Writing Your Job Posting

The job posting on your website should describe the process of applying for participation in the mentorship program. The requirements of the mentor and mentee roles need to be clear enough to help them decide whether to apply. Ask your applicants to submit their résumé and a cover letter with answers to several very specific questions, such as their goals for the program, their strengths, and their opportunities for growth. We recommend the following guidelines for writing the job posting for your mentorship program.

State Program Goals – Start the job description with a statement about the goals of your mentorship program and include details to create interest in the program.

Describe the Role – Provide prospective mentor and mentee candidates with a realistic expectation of the effort required for participation.

Specify Application Requirements – Ask each prospective mentor and mentee to submit their résumé with a cover letter outlining their goals for participation in the program.

Set Deadline for Submission – Remember to set a deadline for applications submissions. Set the mentor application deadline a month prior to the mentee application deadline.

Sample website content describing the mentorship program and the application process for both mentors and mentees is included below.

20XX <Chapter Name> Mentorship Program

<Chapter Name> is seeking exceptional human resource professionals to participate in our Mentorship Program.

Who We Are:

- The <Chapter Name> mentorship program is a developmental partnership through which the mentor shares their knowledge, skills, information and perspective to foster the professional growth of one mentee.

- The purpose of the mentorship program is to support the chapter's objective of furthering the ongoing enhancement of a dynamic, diverse membership and, as a result, the HR profession through learning and networking.

- We give senior-level HR professionals an opportunity to "give back" to our members and our profession through a one of a kind opportunity for collaboration, goal achievement and problem solving.

Who You Are:

Mentor

You facilitate professional growth for another individual by sharing the knowledge and insights you have learned in your years as a human resources professional. You are able to carry out the responsibilities and meet the requirements listed below:

- Active <Chapter Name> Member

- Minimum of five years of HR experience; this can be a combination of HR management, generalist, consultant, or a specialist role (i.e., benefits, compensation, recruitment, etc.)

- Willingness to make a 10-month commitment, starting in January, to your mentee with at least one hour per month in face-to-face meetings

- Completion of the <Chapter Name> mentorship program progress form after your monthly meetings

- Available by phone and/or email throughout the month to your mentee, typically for non-urgent or not time sensitive consultations

- Attendance at monthly group meetings in addition to regular meetings in smaller mentor sub-groups

- PHR/SPHR or other professional certification preferred, though not required

---

Mentee

You are an achiever seeking developmental advancement through opportunities to learn and excel. You are able to carry out the responsibilities and meet the requirements listed below:

- Active <Chapter Name> member
- Dedicated professional wishing to gain additional knowledge and information in Human Resources
- Willingness to make a 10-month commitment, starting in January, to your mentor with at least one hour per month in face-to-face meetings
- Completion of the <Chapter Name> mentorship program progress form after monthly meetings
- Attendance at monthly group meetings in addition to face-to-face meetings with your mentor

How to apply:

If you believe you are the right individual to fill one of these roles, please submit your cover letter and current résumé to mentors@<Chapter Name>.org.

Your cover letter should include:

- Your name and any professional designations
- Contact phone number(s)
- Email address(es)
- Home/work addresses
- Employer name
- A description of your Human Resources background
- Three goals you have for the Mentorship Program
- Important aspects you are looking for in a mentor/mentee partner
- Your three greatest strengths and three areas that need most improvement

Mentors: Please include in the subject line: "20XX <Chapter Name> Mentorship Program – Mentor Application". Deadline for submitting your cover letter and resume is **December 7, 20XX.**

Mentees: Please include in the subject line: "20XX <Chapter Name> Mentorship Program – Mentee Application". Deadline for submitting your cover letter and resume is **January 11, 20XX.**

Please Note:
For the 20XX <Chapter Name> Mentorship Program we will be accepting a maximum of 15 mentors and 15 mentees.
Apply now!

Note: This form is included in Appendix B: Marketing.

Where to Market?

So, where should you promote your new mentorship program?

Website

If you have a chapter website, be sure your mentorship program content is easy to find.

Set up a prominent link on the homepage to the mentorship program information.

This webpage should contain the most detailed information of all the venues you use. You can then link to the mentorship program webpage from other marketing venues, such as e-blasts. The content you create for the website will be available for your use with other marketing strategies.

Email

If you use weekly or monthly email blasts to members, at least one email message should be devoted to announcing and describing the mentorship program and the requirements to participate. If your email frequency is once a month, your marketing plan should begin at least a month before you begin accepting applications; this will allow potential candidates time to think about their schedule for the next year and whether to apply.

Chapter Meeting Announcements

Chapter meeting announcements are a very effective way to market your mentorship program. One reason is that many of the chapter leaders regularly attend the monthly meetings. Announcing the new mentorship program at chapter meetings ensures these leaders will hear and pay attention. Their participation in your program, either as the mentorship program leader, as part of the mentorship committee, or as a mentor, is highly desirable. Another reason chapter meeting announcements are so effective is you can vary the message about the mentorship program each month, which encourages different people to apply.

Social Media

LinkedIn deserves special mention as an extremely effective marketing tool for your mentorship program.

Ask every one of your mentorship committee members to share a link on their personal LinkedIn profile to the mentorship program information on your chapter's website. Many of your chapter members are probably connected on LinkedIn and this is a great way of getting the word out to many people quickly.

People who are active on LinkedIn usually pay attention to their personal brand. They may also follow news and LinkedIn posts related to the Human Resource Management profession.

This works in your favor when publicizing the mentorship program. The mentorship committee members can also take turns posting comments on their personal profile about the benefits of being a mentor for career development.

We also recommend using your chapter's LinkedIn group to publish the requirements to participate in the mentorship program and the announcements made at chapter meetings.

Throughout the year, be sure you announce the beginning of the application period, recognize the candidates who were selected to participate in the mentorship program, and congratulate them at the end on their successful completion of the mentorship program.

If your chapter doesn't have a LinkedIn group, now is a great time to start one with an announcement about the new mentorship program.

Word of Mouth

Word of mouth marketing is tapping into the relationships and networks that naturally exist between the members of your chapter.

The idea is that even before you open the application period for the mentorship program, the "buzz" has already begun about this new program. Chapter members have read about the new program in the email blast, visited the chapter website to get more details, and discussed it with people in their professional network. They heard some of the details in the chapter meeting announcements and they want to know more.

Because the information sources all include the time commitment required and the benefit to their career, chapter members can make their decision and be ready to apply by the time the application period begins.

An important part of successful word of mouth marketing is the use of social networks. Your chapter leaders probably have large professional networks. Be sure the board of directors hears all the details about the mentorship program as they become available. If they know the details of the mentorship program, they will tell their friends.

The novelty of the program will also help word of mouth marketing. People are always interested in being the first to hear about and become a part of something new. Your chapter leadership can be the first wave in in the marketing campaign about the chapter's new program.

As any marketing professional will tell you, word of mouth marketing is one of the most credible forms of advertising. Truthfulness is key in word of mouth advertising – it is important that the time commitment and requirements for the mentorship program be clearly stated *from the beginning*. It builds credibility for the chapter leadership with their friends if they make it known from the onset that participating in the mentorship program is rigorous. This is another reason why all your marketing outlets should use the same messaging.

Setting Up a Point of Contact

Before launching your marketing strategy, designate one committee member to act as the point of contact for the program. You will also need to provide a method of contact, such as a dedicated email address. This address needs to be created during the planning step and monitored by a mentorship committee member throughout the entire year.

Marketing Summary

This chapter illustrates the connection between all the elements necessary to start your mentorship program. The thoroughness of your planning process and the marketing approach you choose both have an enormous impact on the success of your mentorship program.

Don't be too concerned about getting it exact, though. Remember, one of the most important ingredients in a successful mentorship program is *having fun*. Develop and try your marketing ideas, evaluate their success at the end of the program, and make notes about adjustments to include the following year.

Good news – once you have completed all your planning and developed and executed your marketing strategy, you're ready to start recruiting and selecting your mentorship program participants!

Chapter 4
PARTICIPANT SELECTION

After all the planning and marketing activities over the last several months, by now the buzz about the mentorship program should be circulating among your chapter members. Hopefully, people are asking how they can participate in this new chapter program. That's good, because your next step is to find and select the right participants for your mentorship program. It's finally time to begin accepting applications.

This chapter will help you with the selection process for your mentorship program participants. It covers the application process for both mentors and mentees and how to select the participants for your first program.

Selecting Your Mentors

We mentioned previously that the application and acceptance process for both mentors and mentees should be similar to applying for a job. It would be difficult to over-emphasize the importance of the applicants understanding that mental attitude.

Your prospective mentors are applying for a leadership role where they will contribute to the career development of someone less experienced in the HR profession. The role of a mentor is similar to a management position within an organization. For that reason, the mentors' application process should be similar to that of a leadership role within most companies.

Mentor Application Process

If you had multiple volunteers for the role of mentorship program leader, encourage the ones not selected to apply to be mentors. This is a good idea for several reasons. First, it allows chapter members invested in having a mentorship program to be involved and instrumental in the success of the program the first year. Second, their enthusiasm for the mentorship program will be infectious to other program participants. Third, with their experience as mentors they may volunteer to lead the program in succeeding years when your first mentorship program leader steps down.

We recommend starting the application process with the mentors' applications first. By design, the applicants for the role of mentor are senior HR professionals. They are probably very familiar with the recruiting process, and should understand the need to apply for the role of mentor. Because of their HR experience, they may also have suggestions for improving the process by the time the mentee application process begins.

Reviewing Mentor Applications

Once the mentor application period has begun, it's important that every applicant completes all the requirements of the application process. We mention this because in our experience many mentor applicants have been chapter leaders for a long time. Some may have served as chapter president or board members in previous years.

Even though an applicant's qualifications to be a mentor may be familiar to the entire mentorship committee, for consistency's sake all applicants must meet the same requirements. The goal is to make sure the mentorship committee has similar information for all candidates in order to evaluate their applications. Another consideration is that complying with the application requirements demonstrates the mentors are paying attention and are willing to meet the requirements of the mentorship program.

In addition to a current résumé, the content of the cover letter is crucial to an effective evaluation of the applicant's qualifications. Our cover letter requirements are listed below for your reference.

Cover letters need to include:

- Applicant name and title
- Contact phone numbers for both cell and work
- Preferred email address for use while a participant
- Both home and work addresses
- Name of their employer
- Description of their human resources experience
- Three goals for their participation in the mentorship program
- Important characteristics they are looking for in their mentor or mentee partner
- A description of their three greatest strengths and three areas for improvement

All of this information is put to use immediately after the mentor is accepted into the mentorship program. The information provided in the mentors' cover letters is used to create the booklet given to the mentees before the speed mentoring session. They use this information to help them choose a mentor. You can imagine how difficult it would be to collect the information from each participant after the program begins. (For more detail, see *Chapter 5: Speed Mentoring.*)

Time Management and the Application Process

Something to consider in advance is whether to extend the application process for a mentor who wants to participate but just can't get their application submitted by the deadline. It may sound judgmental, but we have found this problem to be another example of someone not truly committed to the mentorship program.

We have all been in situations with a deadline staring us in the face, and somehow we still manage to find the time to finish the project in time. This is also true with the mentorship program applications, especially for mentors. There are many variations on the theme of "I don't have time." However, if prospective mentors don't have time to update their résumé and write a cover letter, how will they find the time to commit to the mentorship program? For this reason, we recommend you keep any extensions of the mentor application period to a minimum; our allowance for late applications is usually at most one week.

We have made exceptions to this rule, but it rarely works out well. Mentors who submit their application late frequently have time management issues. Once the program begins, their time management issues affect their mentee and the other mentorship program participants, making it everyone's problem. By then the trust and relationships among the participants has begun to erode. In the end, no one wins.

It's Not a Popularity Contest – It's also critical that the decision about accepting a particular mentor to participate in the program is not based on popularity. The decision about their acceptance as a mentor must be based on their willingness to commit the time and energy to comply with the program requirements. By clearly stating the application process and following up with mentors who submit incomplete applications, the mentorship committee sets the expectation early on that compliance with the requirements of the mentorship program is crucial.

We've learned through experience that mentors who feel they can skirt the rules with their application are not as committed to the mentorship program. Their lack of commitment becomes more and more obvious throughout the course of the year. It usually leads to them skipping meetings or leaving the program early. Either of these behaviors creates annoyance among the mentorship participants who are attending the meetings and keeping their commitments, and leaves their mentee with an extremely poor mentoring experience.

Schedule Interviews as Applications are Received – As you start receiving mentor applications, review them right away and schedule interviews to determine if the candidates qualify for the mentorship program. Setting the expectation in advance that mentor applicants will be interviewed prior to being selected is helpful. That way they will be expecting your email requesting a meeting to discuss their application. Depending on the number of mentor applications, you may decide to include all the mentorship committee members in the process of interviewing the mentor applicants. If you have just a few mentor applications, for the sake of consistency it might be best for one person to interview all the mentor applicants. Below is a sample email message you can use to acknowledge receipt of their application to become a mentor, and request an interview with a mentor candidate.

Thank you for submitting your application to be a mentor in this year's mentorship program. The next step in the process is to meet with one of the mentorship committee members to complete an interview that will determine who will be selected as mentors for this year.

<Mentorship Committee Member> will be contacting you to set up a time for you to meet at your earliest convenience. Thank you for your interest in this program. If you have any questions, please don't hesitate to call me or just reply to this message.

Thank you,

<Mentorship Program Leader>

<Phone number>

Note: This email message is included in Appendix C: Participant Selection

Choose Your Interviewers – When determining who will conduct the interviews, the most important consideration is how quickly the interviews can be completed. We all know the disappointment of waiting weeks to be interviewed for a new job, and then finding out the position is filled. Contacting mentor applicants within a day or two of receiving their application helps to win the mentors' trust from the beginning and communicates that the mentorship committee is responsive to the concerns of the participants.

Complete Interviews within Two to Three Weeks – How quickly the interviews are completed depends on the schedules of the mentorship committee member(s) and the mentor applicants.

Make sure you complete all your mentor interviews within two to three weeks of receiving the application. Taking more than three weeks affects the timing for the mentee selection process and the rest of the mentorship program.

One of the first responsibilities of the mentors who are selected is to interview the mentee applicants. For this reason, all of the mentors need to be selected and on board before you start the mentee application process.

Sometimes one of the mentorship committee members finds it difficult to complete an interview within two or three weeks after receiving an application. Because they participated in setting up the mentorship program schedule, the committee members are very aware of the need to be flexible with their time to schedule and complete the mentor interviews. They understand the time requirements to be a part of the mentorship committee. Even more important, they have already agreed to spend the time needed to plan and run the mentorship program.

The mentorship committee member should be able to offer multiple opportunities over the three-week interview period to schedule an interview with the mentor applicant.

If all the interview times conflict with the schedule of the applicant, it is a good idea for the mentorship committee leader to have a frank conversation with them about the time requirements to participate in the mentorship program.

If the applicant can't find an hour for an interview with a committee member during a three week time period, they may also not have the time required to participate in the mentorship program. It sounds like a small thing to worry about, but we have learned the hard way to pay attention to these details.

Scheduling problems are the number one cause for the relationship between a mentor-mentee pair to fall apart, and it's also the cause of most people dropping out of our mentorship program early.

Determining early in the process who will have difficulty meeting the time requirements of the program is one of the reasons to conduct mentor interviews. It saves everyone a lot of time and disappointment if you can figure out in advance who has problems with time management.

Conducting the Mentor Interviews

The purpose of the mentor applicant interviews is to assess their understanding of what it means to be a mentor and gauge their willingness to commit to the time requirements of the mentorship program. It helps to use a standard list of questions for the mentor applicant interviews. This allows the mentorship committee to compare the results of the applicants' interviews across the board, even if more than one interviewer was involved in the interview process. A list of suggested interview questions for your mentor applicant interviews is below:

1. What motivated you to apply to our program?

2. What do you hope to gain from this experience?

3. How would you describe the role of a mentor? What does the mentoring process look like to you?

4. Tell me about a time you have mentored/coached someone. What was the outcome?

5. Our mentorship program is a big commitment, with group monthly meetings, individual coaching sessions and homework. How do you feel about that?

Scoring the Mentor Applicants

As each mentor applicant interview is completed, the interviewer should send their interview notes to the mentorship program leader for compilation.

Once the mentor applicant interviews have been completed, the mentorship committee should meet to discuss the results and select the mentors who will be invited to participate in the mentorship program that year.

It's best to meet in person, but if that is impossible, there are number of tools available to do a virtual meeting. Schedule the selection meeting as soon as the last interview is over to avoid delaying the start of the mentorship program.

It is very important that the mentorship program leader has everyone's interview notes available for reference during the mentor selection meeting.

To prepare for the meeting, the program leader should put together a spreadsheet with all the applicants' names. Also included should be the selection factors that the mentorship committee considers critical to success in the mentor role. These are the same factors chosen during the planning process. An example of the how the selection spreadsheet might look follows.

Note: This spreadsheet is included in Appendix C: Participant Selection *and can be downloaded from the Resources Download area.*

	Selection Factors								
Mentor Name	Program Commitment	HR Commitment	Relationship Understanding	Personal Responsibility	Self-Improvement	Difficult Conversation	Years HR Experience	TOTAL	Interviewer Comments
Elisa Eckart									
Daron Dasilva									
Joleen Jonason									

Selection Factor	Description
Program Commitment	Has the candidate said they can attend the meetings? Does the candidate understand the overall commitment? Has the candidate ever shown similar commitment to a volunteer or educational program?
HR Profession Commitment	Do the candidate's goals align with a future career in HR? What has the candidate done (so far) to engage in the HR profession (classes, certificate, internship, job, chapter volunteer)?
Understands Mentor-Mentee relationship	Does the candidate understand that mentors are coaches? Has the candidate been in some type of mentoring relationship?
Personal Responsibility	Does the candidate take ownership for his/her own actions?
Self-Improvement	Has the candidate exhibited an interest in learning (continuing with school, classes, projects)? Does the candidate seem introspective and committed to self-improvement?
Difficult Conversations	Has the candidate had to deal with emotionally charged or difficult conversations? Does the candidate engage or ignore problems with others?
Comfort Level HR Experience	How many years of hands-on HR experience does the candidate have?

If the selection meeting is done virtually, everyone must have access to a computer with screen sharing capability. The mentorship program leader is responsible for setting up the meeting and making sure everyone understands and can use this option. Using this method to hold the meeting will accommodate the visual learners on the mentorship committee. Everyone can view the spreadsheet with the scoring for all the applicants at the same time.

The meeting format should be a discussion facilitated by the mentorship program leader. As each applicant is discussed, the interviewer should present their interview notes and add any additional information that might affect the mentorship committee decision about that applicant.

After the interviewer presents their information on the applicant, the program leader will ask each committee member to rate the applicant on each selection factor.

The rating scale should be a 1 – 5 scale, with 5 being the highest possible score.

The score entered in the spreadsheet for each factor should be the average score of all the committee members. This process is repeated for each selection factor until the total selection score can be computed for that applicant. Repeat this process for each applicant until you have discussed each one.

Scoring Results – At the end of this process, each applicant will have a total selection score.

With the total score for each individual entered for all applicants, sort your spreadsheet by the total scores. This makes it immediately apparent if there are any trends in the applicants' score totals.

We have found there are always a few applicants with a lower total score than the rest of the applicants. After a discussion about the score totals for each applicant, the mentorship committee should decide on the threshold score total for acceptance. That will make it very apparent which applicants will be accepted as mentors in the mentorship program, and who will be notified they were not accepted.

At this point, it's important for the mentorship committee to recall the total number of mentor-mentee pairs planned for the mentorship program that year.

If the total number of mentor applicants is the same or less than the number decided for that year's program, the decision of which mentors to accept is simply a function of which applicants have the highest total selection scores. In that case, the mentorship committee will automatically have the same or less mentors than originally planned for that year.

Fewer Mentor Applicants Than Planned – If there are just enough or slightly fewer mentor applicants than planned, it is perfectly fine to accept all qualified applicants as mentors for your mentorship program. What we don't suggest is you accept mentors into the program without each one going through an application and interview process.

When we began our mentorship program, we weren't sure what factors were important to emphasize in selecting mentors. There wasn't a formal mentor application or interview process established. Through trial and error, we chose the selection factors in the table above as indicative of whether a mentor will attend meetings, be willing to engage in meaningful discussions that contribute to their mentee's professional development, and complete the program. The selection factors you choose for your mentor interviews are up to your mentorship committee. However, we strongly suggest you use some sort of application and interview process from the beginning of your mentorship program.

More Mentor Applicants Than Positions – The most difficult part of selecting mentors happens when you have more qualified mentor applicants than you planned for that year's program. This is when being clear about the time commitment for the program becomes most valuable. If your marketing communications have emphasized the time commitment, it's safe to assume that all the mentor applicants understand in advance the time required to participate in the program.

It's still important to discuss the time commitment in the interview process, but it becomes less of a factor in determining which applicants will be invited to become mentors. In that case, your other selection factors will be even more helpful in determining which applicants to accept.

Again, the individual score totals will help your mentorship committee decide which applicants to accept as mentors.

When in doubt, trust the collective gut of the committee.

There is usually a reason for someone's hesitation about accepting a particular applicant. It is perfectly fine to accept one less mentor than planned. Having one less mentor-mentee pair is much better than accepting a mentor who you aren't sure about, and ending up with an unsuccessful mentor-mentee pair or a mentor who quits the program early.

Late Mentor Applications – What if you receive a late mentor application?

As we frequently say in HR, it depends.

The mentorship committee can decide to include one more mentor that year, even if adding another mentor will go beyond the total number of mentors planned for that year.

What's important is that the late applicant still goes through the mentor interview process with a total selection score above the threshold for acceptance, and the mentorship committee all agree to increase the total number of participants in that year's mentorship program. The good news in this case is that you can accept an additional mentee, because they are chosen after the mentor selection process is completed.

Returning Mentors – While there is no perfect way to determine who to accept as mentors, an application process is the most objective way we know of to choose the mentors for your mentorship program. Using the application process to select mentors is especially important the first year, because you have no mentors from prior years re-applying to the mentorship program.

After their first experience as a mentor, most chapter members self-select whether to continue as a mentor the following year. Since they have already demonstrated their commitment to both the mentorship program and their mentee's professional development, we do not interview mentor applicants if they have already successfully completed the mentorship program in a previous year. Mentors who had a problem with time commitment for the mentorship program usually don't apply to be mentors again. Our return rate for mentors has remained steady at about 50% each year.

Notifying the Mentor Applicants

Once the mentors have been selected, the mentorship program leader notifies all the applicants with a phone call whether they were chosen as mentors for that year's program. As a professional courtesy, the applicants who were not accepted are notified first. If asked, the mentorship program leader explains the reasoning behind the decision not to accept their application for that year.

We suggest that you ask the mentorship program leader to call the prospective mentors to preserve the relationship that exists between them and the chapter. Regardless of whether they were accepted as a mentor, each applicant must be treated as a valuable member of the chapter.

Contact Selected Mentors – After calling the applicants who were not accepted, the mentorship program leader calls the applicants who have been selected as mentors to give them the news and reaffirm their willingness to make the time commitment to the program. The leader also tells them to expect an email with the details for the next step in the process, the mentors' pre-meeting. A sample mentors' pre-meeting message follows.

Congratulations on your selection as a mentor for this year's mentorship program. The first meeting for mentors will be on **<Day of Week>, <Month Day> from <start time> to <end time>** in <room number> at the <location name and web address.>

The <location name> address is:

<Insert location address>

Action Required: Please reply to this message and include in the subject line either "Yes, I will be there" or "No, I won't be there." Please make every effort to attend as we will be coming together as a group for the first time. Please also take a moment to check the address for this location prior to the day of the meeting so you are prepared for the transit time required to be on time.

I hope to see you there – we are really looking forward to this year's mentorship program!

Thank you,
<Mentorship Program Leader>

Note: This email message is included in Appendix C: Participant Selection, *and can be downloaded from the Resources Download area.*

Preparing the Mentors

The first time all the selected mentors meet as a group is at the mentors' pre-meeting. The mentorship committee should provide refreshments for this meeting. Refreshments are a good way to start the mingling process. As people arrive, having food and beverages available helps them relax a bit before the meeting.

Because nearly all the mentorship program meetings are in the evening, tell the participants in advance you will provide refreshments. That way they don't have to rush to get food between leaving work and arriving at the meeting, and it eliminates one reason people might be late.

The mentors' pre-meeting serves several purposes.

It gives the mentors their first opportunity to meet each other and begin developing the relationships with the people they will be spending quite a bit of time with during the next year.

Mentors also enjoy the chance to ask questions of the mentorship program leader about the mentorship program and their participation.

In turn, the mentorship program leader explains the mentee application process and obtains the mentors' agreement to help with the mentee selection process.

If you have more than five mentors in the mentorship program, this is also a good time to form the mentor sub-groups. Mentors usually prefer being in sub-groups created by geographic proximity to their work locations.

The last item on the mentors' pre-meeting agenda is to explain the speed mentoring process.

Now is the time to make sure they have the speed mentoring meeting on their calendars. You should also set the expectation that mentors are required to attend the speed mentoring meeting. You probably won't get much pushback about the attendance requirement. By this time in the process, the idea of doing speed mentoring is intriguing to just about everyone. A sample mentors' pre-meeting agenda follows.

Mentors Get Acquainted Meeting
\<LOCATION NAME\>
\<LOCATION ADDRESS\>

Handouts:

- Agenda
- Mentorship program meeting dates
- Mentorship program requirements
- Mentor/mentee locations
- Mentee interview questions
- Mentee selection factors

Agenda:

6:00 – 6:15 PM   **Mingle and refreshments**

6:15 – 6:20 PM   **Introduction to the mentorship program**
- Purpose of the mentorship program:
    - Further the ongoing enhancement of a dynamic, diverse membership and, as a result, the HR profession through learning and networking
    - Build a stronger HR community
    - Teach other HR professionals how to be "a business partner who specializes" – strategic rather than transactional

---

> **6:20 – 7:00 PM   Mentor introductions**
> - Name
> - Position
> - Interest in the program
> - Personal goal for the program
> - Fun fact about your first HR job
>
>
> **7:00 – 7:30 PM   Announcements, mentor sub-groups and mentee interviews**
> - Introduce mentorship program leader
> - Meeting attendance is mandatory
> - Communicate at the FIRST hint of disengagement ("it takes a village")
> - Form mentor sub-groups (geographically based)
>
>
> **7:30 – 7:45 PM   Next meeting: Speed mentoring on <DATE> @ <TIME>**
> - Bring résumés if desired
> - Treat as an informational interview (but much shorter!)
>
>
> **7:45 – 8:00 PM   Questions / Networking**

Note: This agenda is included in Appendix C: Participant Selection *and can be downloaded from the Resources Download area.*

Handouts

This is a good time to talk about the handouts required for the mentors' pre-meeting. As part of the planning process, the mentorship committee created a document with the program requirements from the application process information on the chapter website. The program meeting dates were also determined during the planning process.

Assign one of your mentorship committee members to coordinate the mentors' pre-meeting, including putting together the handouts listed above, such as the program requirements and mentorship program meeting dates. There are examples of these handouts in the Resources Download area to modify and use in your program.

The mentee interview questions and selection factors are the same as those used for the mentor selection process, so there is no preparation needed to create these handouts. The mentors will recognize the list of questions as the ones asked in their interviews. The list of selection factors will be new to them.

Sometimes it is a little surprising to the mentors that the mentorship committee knows what factors are critical for success as a mentor or mentee. If asked, we tell them the list comes from our observation of successful participants in prior years. Mentors from prior years usually chime in at that point and provide validation of the selection factors for the newer mentors. Since this is the first year of your program, you can always say you modeled the program on another successful mentorship program.

The handout with the mentor and mentee work and home locations is the most crucial handout for the mentors' pre-meeting and can take the most time to prepare. The mentors' work and home cities are available from their application and compiling their information will not take a lot of time unless some of the mentor applications were incomplete.

Tracking down missing information from the participants' applications can be time consuming. They may have just forgotten to include the cities where they work and live. Other participants may be reluctant to divulge this information for privacy reasons. However, it is critical to the success of the program that they share this information with the mentorship committee.

Without knowing where a participant lives or works, it is very difficult to pair them with a mentor or mentee who is geographically compatible for their monthly 1:1 meetings. If you don't have this information in advance, you may end up with one or more mentor-mentee pairs who live and work 30 – 50 miles from each other. When this happens, the mentorship pair might try to reassure you it won't be a problem and promise to meet every month.

No matter how motivated someone is, it is nearly impossible to commit to and participate in eight or nine monthly meetings that require you to drive 30, 40 or even 50 miles. Instead, it is very likely that those mentorship pairs will stop having their monthly meetings at some point in the program. They may quit the mentorship program early or just drift out of contact with each other long before the program ends. To solve for this problem in advance, make it a requirement of your mentorship program that every participant disclose the name of the cities where they live and work.

In our experience, as soon as you tell the participants you only need the names of the cities where they live and work, and that you're asking for this information to save them time, they see the logic in providing the information. The location where each participant lives and works completes the first part of this handout.

To add the mentee applicants' geographical information to your mentors' pre-meeting handout, the mentee application period must be ending or just completed, with all or most of the applications received. For this reason, the beginning and ending of the mentee application period should be carefully timed around the date of the mentors' pre-meeting. With the mentors doing the interviews for the mentee applicants, they need the geographical information so they can choose which mentee applicants they volunteer to interview.

Fortunately, a lot of mentees send in their applications during the mentors' application period because they are so excited that the mentorship program is (finally) getting started. Feel free to add each mentee's location information to your handout as you receive their application. That way you can finalize the locations handout the day before the mentors' pre-meeting by adding the location information from the last few mentee applications.

Interviewing Mentee Applicants

The most important part of the mentors' pre-meeting is explaining the mentee application, interview, and selection process to the mentors.

While you can encourage the mentors to take responsibility for the mentee applicant interviews, it isn't absolutely necessary. It does help the mentorship committee members who have worked diligently up to this point. They really appreciate the chance to share the effort of getting the mentorship program started with the mentors.

The mentors like doing the interviews – for them it's like getting a glimpse behind the curtain of how the mentorship program is set up and what the coming year holds for them as mentors.

Another benefit of the mentors taking responsibility for the mentee applicant interviews is their increased commitment to the mentorship program.

The mentors enjoy meeting with the mentee applicants. As experienced HR professionals, they are familiar with the recruitment process.

Most of the mentors are excited at this point and interested in assuming the responsibilities they agreed to when they applied to be part of the program.

Also, to receive the full five HRCI recertification credits for their participation in the mentorship program, the mentors need to be involved early so their volunteer time spans as much of the year as possible.

For all these reasons, we recommend asking the mentors to complete the interviews for the mentee applicants rather than have the mentorship committee members do them.

It takes extra effort during the mentors' pre-meeting to communicate the interview process and selection criteria to the mentors who volunteer to do the mentees' interviews.

It also requires more coordination on the part of the mentorship committee to be sure the mentors forward their interview notes to the mentorship program leader as soon as possible in preparation for the mentee selection meeting.

Just as in the mentor application process, it's important that the mentee interviews are completed quickly to avoid delaying the start of the rest of the mentorship program meetings.

Selecting Your Program Mentees

In applying to the mentorship program, the mentee applicants are asking to be considered for a role that offers them significant opportunities for both personal and career development. Even with less HR or work experience, they need to take the application process as seriously as the mentors. People who truly value the opportunity of being a mentee will view the mentorship application and selection process as though it is the next level up in their career. You should definitely see that point of view reflected in the care they take in preparing and submitting their application for the mentorship program.

The process for selecting mentees for your mentorship program is similar to the mentor selection process. In this part of the process, the mentors selected in the previous step conduct the interviews of the mentees.

Mentee Application Process

It may seem redundant, but it bears repeating that all mentee applicants for the mentorship program must meet the same requirements.

This is as true for the mentee applicants as it is for the mentors.

The goal is to make sure the mentorship committee has similar information for all candidates in order to evaluate their applications. Another consideration is that their compliance with the application requirements demonstrates they are paying attention and will meet the requirements of the mentorship program.

In addition to a current résumé, the content of the cover letter is crucial to effective evaluation of the applicant's qualifications. The cover letter requirements are listed below again for your reference.

Cover letters must include:

- Applicant name and title
- Contact phone numbers for both cell and work
- Preferred email address for use while a participant
- Both home and work addresses
- Name of their employer
- Description of their human resources experience
- Three goals for their participation in the mentorship program
- Important characteristics they are looking for in their mentor or mentee partner
- A description of their three greatest strengths and three areas for improvement

One of the motivations for starting a mentorship program is that less experienced HR professionals want and need an opportunity for guidance from someone more experienced in human resource management. If your chapter is like ours, there are always individuals asking how they can find someone to help answer questions about situations that come up in their workplace.

For this reason, you will probably have more mentee applicants than available positions in your mentorship program. We always have more mentees applying to the mentorship program than mentors available to work with them. Because of this, it's important that your mentorship committee stick with their original plan for the number of mentor-mentee pairs to have in the program, especially the first year. One of the hardest parts in your mentorship program will be telling some of your mentee applicants they weren't selected for the program.

There is a usually a flurry of mentee applications as soon as you begin accepting them. Since you will most likely have more applications than spaces for mentees in the program, don't worry about the length of your mentee application period. One or two weeks should be more than enough time. Again, it's important to acknowledge receipt of the applications and start interviewing applicants as soon as possible.

Missed Application Deadline

One challenge you may have is letting people know they missed the application window to apply to be a mentee in the mentorship program. To avoid this, use every available channel of communication to make it perfectly clear exactly when the mentee application process opens and closes.

The most likely scenario is that your prospective mentees read the description of how to apply on the website and have their application ready to submit as soon as the application period begins. Some of them submit their application early to be sure they are considered for the program.

If they send in their application early, it's important to acknowledge receipt of their application, and set the expectation that submitting their application early does not change the time frame for mentee applicants to be interviewed.

If you receive a mentee's application early, let them know when the application period for mentees begins, and that they will be contacted after that to schedule an interview for the program.

Conducting Mentee Interviews

You can use the same set of questions for the mentee interviews as for the mentor interviews. The selection criteria are also the same.

The biggest difference is that you should ask the mentor completing the interview to send their scores for each selection factor for the applicant to the mentorship program leader the same day they complete the interview, along with their interview notes.

Once again, the mentorship program leader compiles the scores for all the prospective mentees before the mentorship committee meets to select the mentees for the program.

Perhaps because the mentee applicants have less work experience, they are frequently very nervous about being interviewed by one of the mentors.

For this reason, we stopped calling the mentee applicant interviews an "interview". We now call them "mentor advisor meetings".

This way the mentee applicants are less nervous and more likely to ask questions of the mentor during the meeting.

Even without characterizing it as an interview, the mentors still get enough information about the mentees during the meeting to make a recommendation on whether to accept them into the mentorship program.

The remainder of the mentee selection process is the same as the process for selecting the mentors. As soon as the selection meeting is held, the mentees are notified by a telephone call from the mentorship program leader whether they were accepted into the mentorship program for that year.

As with the mentors, the applicants who were not accepted are notified first.

If asked, the mentorship program leader explains the reasoning behind the decision not to accept their application for that year. This is done by the mentorship program leader to preserve the relationship between the applicant and the chapter. Regardless of whether they were accepted as a mentee, each applicant must be treated as a valuable member of the chapter.

Contact Mentees Not Accepted

Mentees who aren't accepted frequently ask if they can apply the following year to the mentorship program.

For many reasons, we recommend that your answer to this question is, "Yes."

No one can predict the changes that can happen in a year. For some people, the additional time brings enough life experience that they are better prepared the following year to get the most from the program. Others use that year to move their HR career to the next level or independently find a mentor in their workplace, and may not feel the same need to apply for a formal mentorship program when the opportunity comes around again.

Contact Selected Mentees

After calling the applicants who were not accepted, the mentorship program leader calls the applicants selected as mentees to give them the news. An important part of this call is reaffirming their willingness to make the time commitment to the program. When the mentee applicants are notified of their acceptance, you should also set the expectation that they will receive a message with the details for the next step in the process, the mentees' pre-meeting. A sample mentees' pre-meeting message follows.

Congratulations on your selection as a mentee for this year's mentorship program. The first meeting for mentees will be on **<Day of Week>, <Month Day> from <start time> to <end time>** in <room number> at <location name>. The <location name> address is:

<Insert location address>

Action item: Please reply to this message and include in the subject line either "Yes, I will be there" or "No, I won't be there". Please make every effort to attend as we will be coming together as a group for the first time. Please also take a moment to check the address for this location prior to the day of the meeting so you are prepared for the transit time required to be on time.

I hope to see you there – we are looking forward to this year's mentorship program!

Thank you,
<Mentorship Program Leader>

Note: This email message is included in Appendix C: Participant Selection *and can be downloaded from the Resources Download area.*

Preparing the Mentees

The mentees' pre-meeting serves several purposes.

It gives the mentees their first opportunity to meet each other and begin developing relationships with the people they will be spending time with over the next year.

The handouts for the mentee's pre-meeting are the same as the ones created for the mentors' pre-meeting, so the biggest part of preparing for the meeting is printing extra copies for the mentees.

As for the mentors, the mentorship committee provides refreshments for the mentees' pre-meeting. The mentees are very excited as they arrive, and the food and beverages help them relax somewhat before the meeting.

Tell your participants in advance that you will provide refreshments. When they know food will be available, it eliminates one reason they might be late to the meeting.

One difference between the mentors and mentees at this point is that the mentees have a sense of getting through the first hurdle. The feeling is similar to applying for a job and being selected for an interview. They are excited to be a part of the mentorship program and always have questions about how the program works. The pre-meeting gives them the chance to get answers to their questions. They also get to hear the answers to everyone else's concerns.

We suggest that at the mentees' pre-meeting you spend some time re-emphasizing the time commitment of the mentorship program. It is always exciting to start a new phase of your career, and the mentees may have heard from a variety of sources about the benefits of being a part of the program. Spend some time in this meeting going over the details about the time commitment. This ensures everyone understands the investment they will need to make to get to the next level of their career.

The last item on the mentees' pre-meeting agenda is the same as in the mentors' pre-meeting: explaining the speed mentoring process, setting the expectation that they are required to attend, and ensuring they already have the speed mentoring meeting on their calendars. A sample mentees' pre-meeting agenda follows.

Mentees Get Acquainted Meeting
\<LOCATION NAME\>
\<LOCATION ADDRESS\>

Handouts:

- Agenda
- Mentorship program meeting dates
- Mentorship program requirements

Agenda

6:00 – 6:15 PM: **Mingle and refreshments**

-

6:15 – 6:20 PM   **Introduction to the mentorship program**

- Purpose: "Further the ongoing enhancement of a dynamic, diverse membership and, as a result, the HR profession through learning and networking"
- Build a stronger HR community
- Teach other HR professionals how to be "a business partner who specializes" – strategic rather than transactional

6:20 – 7:00 PM   **Mentee introductions**

- Name
- Position
- Interest in the program
- Personal goal for the program
- Fun fact about your first job

7:00 – 7:30 PM   Announcements

- Introduce Mentorship Program Chair
- Meeting attendance is mandatory
- Communicate at the FIRST hint of disengagement ("it takes a village")

7:30 – 7:45 PM   Next meeting: Speed mentoring on <DATE> @ <TIME>

- Bring résumés if desired
- Treat as an informational interview (but much shorter!)

7:45 – 8:00 PM   Questions / Networking

Note: This agenda is included in Appendix C: Participant Selection.

Selection Summary

In this chapter, we covered the process for screening applicants and selecting your mentors and mentees. You now know how to:

- Conduct the application process for both your mentors and mentees
- Select your mentor and mentee candidates
- Prepare the candidates for participation in your mentorship program

At conclusion of the selection process, your program participants are selected and you're ready to move on to the speed mentoring session.

Selection Activities

The following table provides a quick list of the steps for selecting and preparing your mentor and mentee candidates.

Step #	Process	Description	Assigned To
Step 1	**Select mentors**		
	Process mentor applications	• Screen mentor applications	Committee members
	Interview mentor applicants	• Conduct mentor interviews • Score applicants/send scores and notes to leader	Committee members
		• Compile scores and notes	Program leader
	Select mentors	• Meet to discuss and select mentors	Program leader and committee members

Step #	Process	Description	Assigned To
	Notify mentor applicants	• Call all applicants • Send acceptance email to mentors	Program leader
	Mentors' pre-meeting	• Arrange refreshments • Prepare agenda • Prepare handouts • Bring printed handouts	Committee members
		• Conduct pre-meeting	Program leader
Step 2	**Select mentees**		
	Process mentee applications	• Screen mentee applications	Committee members
	Interview mentee applicants	• Conduct interviews • Score mentee applicants • Send scores and notes to mentorship program leader	Mentors
		• Compile scores and notes	Program leader
	Select mentees	• Meet to discuss and select mentees	Program leader and committee members
	Notify mentee applicants	• Call all applicants • Send email to accepted applicants	Program leader
	Conduct mentees' pre-meeting	• Arrange refreshments • Prepare agenda • Prepare handouts • Bring printed handouts	Committee members
		• Conduct the meeting	Program leader

Selection Roles and Responsibilities

Role	Responsibility
Program leader	• Conduct selection meetings • Lead the mentorship committee in selecting participants • Compile interview scores and notes • Notify applicants of acceptance or non-acceptance • Communicate pre-meeting information to selected mentors • Communicate pre-meeting information to selected mentees • Conduct pre-meetings
Mentorship committee members	• Process mentor applications • Interview mentor applicants • Select mentors • Prepare for mentors' pre-meeting • Process mentee applications • Assign mentors to interview mentee applicants • Select mentees • Prepare for mentees' pre-meeting
Mentors	• Interview mentee applicants • Send interview notes and selection scores for each completed mentee interview to mentorship program leader

Chapter 5
SPEED MENTORING

Everyone who has been a part of the speed mentoring process in our mentorship program would probably agree that it includes just a little bit of the unexpected. It's hard to describe unless you've participated in it. Afterwards, nearly everyone looks back and thinks, "That was fun!"

What is speed mentoring?

For most people, the phrase invokes the experience or image in movies of speed dating. This is intentional.

Speed mentoring is literally the process of spending a few minutes talking with someone in a timed conversation. When the end is announced, one of you moves to the next seat over, and you both begin the process again with a different person. It's a little like the children's game of musical chairs.

The idea may seem far-fetched that spending 5 – 7 minutes with someone would allow you to determine if you want to spend many hours over the next year mentoring or being mentored by that person.

Yet, year after year we have seen that speed mentoring is the best way to accomplish the selection process and to find out which mentors and mentees are best suited to work together.

Speed mentoring elevates the process of pairing the mentors and mentees from using just the logic and reasoning of the mentorship committee members to including the judgment and preferences of all the mentorship program participants that year.

The speed mentoring process exponentially increases the chances for success of your mentor-mentee pairs over the course of the year. This chapter walks you through the steps to set up and conduct your speed mentoring meeting and to determine your mentor-mentee pairs.

Importance of the Mentor-Mentee Pairs Selection

It's probably clear by this point that the mentor-mentee pairing process is one of the most important parts of the program.

Get it right, and the mentee is positioned for success in their HR career. Get it wrong, and the mentee loses the opportunity for career development and wastes the time they invested in the mentoring program.

The same is true for your mentors.

With the right mentee, mentors have the opportunity to develop a relationship where they can make a significant contribution to the HR profession by mentoring a member of the next generation of HR leaders.

In an ineffective mentor-mentee relationship, the mentor becomes frustrated. They see that their recommendations aren't being acted on, because the mentee doesn't see the mentor's recommendations as valuable. As a result, the mentee may completely cut off communication with their mentor.

In one of our most extreme examples, a mentee moved out-of-state without telling anyone in the mentorship program. The mentor learned of their mentee's new job and location when the mentee changed their LinkedIn profile!

Another incentive to make sure your mentorship pairings are successful is that when the mentor-mentee relationship works, mentors see the results in the life of their mentee, and often become long-term advocates of the mentorship program. They participate in the program year after year because they see the benefit of their time investment.

The fact that they receive HRCI recertification credit for their participation in a mentorship program is usually secondary; their satisfaction comes directly from witnessing their mentee's progress throughout that year and their subsequent career. Many of your participants will probably develop a long-term professional relationship with their mentor or mentee.

The reverse is also true, especially in the mentor's first year of the program. If the match is not paired well and the mentor feels they did not contribute to their mentee's development during the program, many mentors will not participate in the mentorship program the following year.

The hidden cost of ineffective mentor-mentee pairings is the constant need to recruit new mentors in order to continue the program each year.

Everything you do to improve the quality of the relationships in your mentor-mentee pairs is entirely worth the effort. It is one of the best ways to sustain your mentorship program. A successful mentorship program provides enormous benefits for the participants, allowing it to become a critical component in the growth and success of your chapter.

Speed Mentoring: The Beginning

In the third year of our mentorship program, we had several mentor-mentee pairs that weren't well matched. It was clear early on these relationships were not successful. The mentors involved reported their mentees had stopped making an effort to achieve their goals for the program, and one mentee simply stopped talking to their mentor.

In our end-of-program brainstorming session about improvements to make for the following year, one of the mentors suggested we add "speed dating" as a part of the matching process for the mentors and mentees. We all laughed, as she intended, but it was the right idea at exactly the right time.

Given time for reflection, the mentorship committee decided to try speed mentoring as part of selecting the mentor-mentee pairs for the mentorship program the next year. We designed the process just like a speed dating session.

Fortunately, the participants were willing to suspend judgment about the process the first year we tried it. The speed mentoring session was wildly successful and everyone enjoyed it immensely. Even the most introverted participants mentioned how much fun it was to talk with 15 complete strangers in the same evening.

The year before we introduced speed mentoring, one-third of the mentor-mentee pairs experienced early closure (the relationships ended before the official program ended).

In contrast, the first year we tried speed mentoring only one mentor-mentee pair of the fifteen pairs in the program experienced early closure. By the end of the mentorship program that year it was obvious that the quality of the mentor-mentee relationships was much improved.

Since the only change we made to the program that year was the addition of speed mentoring, we knew we had added a completely new dimension to the program with this one change. That was enough for us to declare speed mentoring a success, and we have achieved similar results every year since that time.

Speed Mentoring: The Process

Planning is the most important factor for success in your first speed mentoring session. Communication with all the mentorship program participants about how the process works is the second most important factor for success. Both of these factors are interrelated.

Since "speed" is an integral part of the process, the speed mentoring session needs to be well planned to keep the momentum going during the entire meeting.

To achieve that speed, participants must understand their role in each step of the process. Once everyone's questions have been answered and they understand what to do, everyone can "go with the flow" and have a good time getting to know each other.

Preparing for the Speed Mentoring Meeting

As soon as the mentorship program participants have been selected, the committee members need to prepare for the speed mentoring meeting.

Ideally, the preparations will be completed two weeks prior to the speed mentoring meeting.

At minimum, the preparations need to be completed a week prior to the speed mentoring meeting.

This includes ensuring the room is available, that all participants plan to attend, and that all participants receive the meeting materials in advance of the meeting.

Although one person can do all the speed mentoring preparations for 5 - 10 mentor-mentee pairs, this is where it really helps to have a mentorship committee who can divide the work to prepare for the meeting. Below is a list of the preparations that need to be done for the speed mentoring session.

1. Confirm the location and availability of the meeting facility
2. Schedule the meeting
3. Monitor meeting acceptances
4. Arrange refreshment for the meeting
5. Prepare the mentor and mentee booklets
6. Email the mentor booklets to the mentees
7. Email the mentee booklets to the mentors

Speed Mentoring Booklets

As mentioned before, during the process of applying for the mentorship program, all applicants were asked send in their résumé and a cover letter describing their strengths, opportunities for improvement, and goals for the program. This information in each participant's application is used in the preparations for the speed mentoring process. A short bio is created from each person's cover letter to include in the speed mentoring booklet.

About a week before the speed mentoring session, each mentee is sent a booklet with the pertinent information for all the mentors, and each mentor receives a booklet with the pertinent information for all the mentees.

The booklets become their reference for use during the speed mentoring process. This way each participant begins the speed mentoring process with some basic knowledge about each person they talk to.

It also gives them a beginning for their conversations. And since each conversation lasts less than 10 minutes, having the person's bio available saves time by eliminating the need to ask basic questions, such as the other person's name, current job, etc.

Note: See Appendix D: Speed Mentoring Session *for a sample mentor and mentee booklet.*

Create and email your booklets at least one week before the speed mentoring session. The program leader's message when sending the booklets should set the expectation that mentors and mentees need to review the information before arriving at the meeting. In your message to the mentors, make sure you note that their input after the speed mentoring session about the pairing process is highly encouraged. Ask them to plan their time that evening so they can stay for a few minutes after the meeting is over to help with tabulating the ballots.

Some participants choose to be prepared and bring a printed copy of the booklet with them to the meeting. Even so, it's still a good idea for the mentorship committee to bring enough printed copies of both booklets to the meeting for all the participants to use during the speed mentoring session.

Speed Mentoring Ballots

Before the speed mentoring session, prepare two ballots: one with the names of all the mentors, and another with the names of all the mentees. Listing the names in alphabetical order will make it easier for the participants to vote for their top three mentor or mentee choices at the end of the speed mentoring session.

Once the speed mentoring conversations are finished, each participant must vote for their top three choices for their mentee or mentor.

Give participants the chance to vote immediately after the final speed mentoring conversations while their impressions are fresh. If they are indecisive, have them refer to their speed mentoring booklet and notes to refresh their memory. The voting process ensures their preferences are communicated. Using ballots is familiar to most people, and is a quick and easy way to do this.

Bring enough printed copies of the ballots for each group, plus a few extras. At least one person will change their mind and ask for a new ballot. If you have extras, it will make their choices that much easier to read than if there are multiple numbers that must be interpreted next to the names on the ballot.

Note: See Appendix D: Speed Mentoring Session *for a sample mentee and mentor ballot.*

Room Layout

The meeting format for the speed mentoring meeting is structured but not complicated. The easiest way to arrange the seating for the speed mentoring process is to position tables along three sides of a large rectangle. Chairs are then placed around the outside and inside perimeters of the tables, with an equal number of chairs on both the inside and the outside of the tables.

When they arrive, the participants already know their status as either a mentee or a mentor.

Ask the mentors to seat themselves around the outside of the tables, and tell the mentees to seat themselves around the inside of the tables.

During the speed mentoring process, mentors should stay seated in their original chair throughout the session. Mentees will change chairs to the next position and next mentor after each round. Because the mentees will keep changing positions, you don't need to assign seats for the participants.

Leading the Speed Mentoring Session

The Clock is Ticking! – The mentorship program leader and some of the mentorship committee members may also be mentors, so it's important that the entire mentorship committee understands how the speed mentoring session is supposed to proceed.

You will need a volunteer to direct the speed mentoring process, monitoring the length of each speed mentoring segment to keep things moving. The easiest way to find a volunteer to do the timing is to have the mentorship committee ask someone in their network.

Now that we've been doing the speed mentoring for several years, we usually recruit a former mentee. They love being a part of the process again, and know in advance exactly how the speed mentoring meeting needs to be structured.

Depending on the size of your group, each conversation should last 5 – 7 minutes, with 1 minute between conversations for participants to jot down any notes and thoughts about the person they just interviewed.

In addition, you may need to take a short (5 minute) break about halfway through the speed mentoring process. If you have less than 10 pairs our recommendation is to continue straight through. It's fairly difficult after a break to get everyone re-focused on their speed mentoring conversations.

Keep it Moving! – One of the most difficult things to manage during the speed mentoring process is making sure mentees move to the next seat when time is called to end each conversation.

Conversely, it's important to wait until everyone is in their correct seat before you start the timer for a new conversation round. No one likes having their time cut short during a segment because someone didn't change seats in time, and these delays affect everyone's participation.

Decide carefully on your choice of facilitator for the speed mentoring session. The facilitator needs to take charge of the meeting, speak loudly to be heard above the 10 – 30 people talking during the speed mentoring conversations, and do whatever is needed to get the mentees to move to their new seat when the timer goes off.

The facilitator is there to be sure each conversation starts on time. After the first few rounds, the participants usually get into the rhythm, and the speed mentoring session moves along at a good pace.

Cast Your Ballots! – After going around the room, the mentees will eventually find themselves seated again in front of the first person they interviewed. At that point, the speed mentoring conversations stop and the voting begins.

The facilitator tells everyone that they have five minutes to complete their ballot. Tell each participant to mark their ballot with a "1" next to the name of their first choice, a "2" next to the name of their second choice, and a "3" next to the name of their third choice. Designate someone to be the ballot collector so everyone knows where to hand in their ballot. After they turn in their ballots the mentees should leave for the evening.

Occasionally a participant wants to provide a rank order for all the choices on their ballot. Discourage this practice; it actually makes the pairing process much more difficult. When 5 – 15 people give you their choices in ranked order for another 5 – 15 people, the number of possible combinations expands out of control. Limit people to their top three choices and force them to choose. This will make the pairing process much easier.

The Pairing Process

Now the fun of matching mentors with mentees begins!

It works best if you select the mentor-mentee pairings using the mentors' preferences for their mentee. The mentors are usually experienced enough to have a good understanding of which mentee is the best match for their strengths and HR experience. Since they met and talked with all the mentees that evening, their views about each mentee are invaluable in determining the right mentor for each mentee.

Having the mentors stay for the pairing process helps assure their buy-in for the mentee chosen for them, and allows them to contribute their perspective on who might be the best mentor for an individual mentee. To accomplish the pairing process, have the mentors and the mentorship committee sit around a table where they can see and hear each other.

Separate the ballots into two stacks, with the mentees' ballots in one stack and the mentors' ballots in another stack. Before the meeting begins, designate one mentorship committee member to be in charge of the mentors' ballots. Select another mentorship committee member to review the mentees' ballots.

Start the process by having the committee member read one of the mentor's top three mentee choices aloud. As they do, the committee member with the mentee ballots looks over the mentees' ballots to see who picked that mentor. The pairing process works like this:

1. A mentorship committee member selects a mentor ballot and reads their #1 choice for a mentee aloud.

2. The mentorship committee member with the mentees' ballots finds the ballot of that mentee and reviews their choices to see if the mentor is one of their top three choices.

3. If the mentor and the mentee have selected each other as one of each other's top three choices, the two ballots are paper clipped together, and set aside as a mentor-mentee pair.

4. If the mentor's #1 mentee choice did not select that mentor, repeat step 2 with the mentor's #2 mentee choice.

5. If the mentor's #2 mentee choice did not select that mentor, repeat step 2 with the mentor's #3 mentee choice.

6. If none of the top three mentee choices of the mentor selected them as one of their three choices, put the mentor's ballot aside, and move on to the next mentor ballot.

After going through all of the mentors' ballots the first time, usually about half of the mentors will be matched with a mentee of their choice.

Then the committee member in charge of the mentee ballots should select a mentee ballot from those left unpaired, and ask the mentors their opinion on the best mentor for each unpaired mentee. You can usually complete all but one or two of the mentor-mentee pairs this way.

At the end, the ballots for one or two mentees and mentors who have not chosen each other may still be left unpaired. Use the combined wisdom of the mentors and the mentorship committee to complete the pairings.

After you are finished with this step, one of the mentorship committee members should take charge of the ballots. They should send the preliminary list of the mentor-mentee pairings to the committee members and the mentors, with a request that the committee be notified of any additional information that comes to light after everyone has had a chance to review the list and send their comments to the mentorship committee.

The timeline for submitting any additional information should be limited to two days at most. This helps the mentorship committee to quickly finalize the list of mentor-mentee pairs.

Then the individual pairs are notified they were selected to work together that year. Send out the final mentor-mentee matches to everyone in the mentorship program as soon as possible, and no later than one week before the training session. This will allow them time to meet once before the training session if they would like.

Announce Mentor-Mentee Pairs

As soon as the list of mentor-mentee pairs in finalized, the mentorship program leader notifies all the participants via email about their partner for the duration of the mentorship program. Send the message to the mentor and mentee copied together. The tone of this message should be celebratory.

After weeks of anticipation, applying to the program, and completing the speed mentoring process, the participants finally know who will be their partner in the mentoring program for the coming year. Your notification messages might begin like this:

> "Congratulations! You have been matched for the 20XX <Chapter Name> Mentorship Program. You were matched together based on your requested match and your goals for the program."

Note: This email message is included in Appendix D: Speed Mentoring Session.

The rest of your email announcement should remind participants about the training session date, time, location, and preparation needed.

Speed Mentoring Summary

Speed Mentoring Activities

Speed Mentoring Session		
Prepare	Confirm location and availability of venue	Committee member
	Schedule the meeting	Committee member
	Monitor meeting acceptances	Committee member
	Arrange meeting refreshments	Committee member
	Prepare the mentor and mentee booklets	Committee member
Communicate	Notify participants of speed mentoring session details	Committee member
	Email mentor booklets to the mentees	Committee member
	Email mentee booklets to the mentors	Committee member
Conduct speed mentoring session	Conduct mentor-mentee interviews	Volunteer (non-participant)
	Collect ballots	Committee member
Match mentors and mentees	Initial ballot matches	Program leader, committee members, and mentors
	Send email to mentors with preliminary pairs for review	Program leader
	Review, update, and finalize mentor-mentee pairs	Program leader and committee members
Announce mentor-mentee pairs	Send confirmation email to mentors and mentees, including contact info and training session details	Program leader

Speed Mentoring Roles and Responsibilities

Role	Responsibility
Mentorship program leader	• Conduct the speed mentoring session • Lead the mentorship committee members and mentors in matching process • Communicate initial pair matches to mentorship committee and mentors • Weigh feedback on and finalize mentor-mentee pairs • Announce final mentor-mentee pairs
Mentorship committee members	• Prepare for speed mentoring session • Participate in speed mentoring session • Assist with mentor-mentee pairing
Mentors	• Participate in the speed mentoring session • Assist with initial mentor-mentee matches • Review the draft mentor-mentee pairs and provide feedback
Mentees	• Participate in the speed mentoring process

Chapter 6
TRAINING SESSION

For your mentors and mentees, the training session will feel like the beginning of their mentorship program. The program leader and mentorship committee have been working for months to get the program off the ground, but the mentorship program doesn't really seem like it starts until the participants are selected and the mentors and mentees are matched. Then and only then can the mentoring relationships start. That is the true beginning of the mentorship program.

The training is one of the focal points of your mentorship program.

Take this time to communicate the theoretical framework of your mentorship program to all the participants. Knowing *why* the mentoring program has more formality will help the participants understand some of the program requirements. Understanding the theory behind the mentoring relationship also gives them a framework to use in creating their own mentoring relationships.

Another reason most of the participants see the training session as the beginning of the program is that it's their first chance to spend more than a few minutes with their mentor or mentee.

It's also the first time everyone in the program interacts as a group. Even though all the participants meet each other at the speed mentoring session, that meeting is highly structured. The training session is also structured, but you should build time into the agenda so all the participants can start getting to know each other.

This chapter walks you through preparing for the training session, conducting the training session, and how to follow up with your participants after the training session.

Preparing for the Training Session

The mentorship committee member organizing the training session needs to for plan a three-hour group meeting with refreshments, handouts, and a PowerPoint presentation using a projector.

Training Session Objectives

Before the training session takes place, you need to be sure all the participants understand the objectives and expectations for the meeting. The objectives for the training session are:

- Inform the program participants about the theoretical framework for the mentorship program
- Review the key agreements needed to assure success in the mentoring relationship
- Identify and begin developing the networks and chapter support available for the mentorship pairs
- Identify and plan the next steps for each mentorship pair

Participant Requirements

The committee member coordinating the training session should also make sure the participants understand their part of the training session. Since this is the first of the mentorship program meetings, is critical to be clear about these expectations of all the mentorship program participants:

Attendance – The success of the training session begins with setting expectations during the application process that attendance at the training session is mandatory. As soon as the mentors and mentees are selected, even before the speed mentoring session, a mentorship committee member must send a meeting request with the details of the training session to all the participants to make sure it is on their calendars. The meeting request should contain both the date and time of the meeting as well as the address and directions for how to get there. It's usually never a problem to confirm attendance with the mentees. They are excited and ready to start their journey of professional development.

Returning Mentors – Some mentors who participate in the mentorship program every year may question the value of making time to be at the training session when they are already familiar with the theoretical basis of the program. It's important that even the returning mentors attend each year's training session. The first year of your mentorship program this won't be an issue. However, it could become important in future years.

The mentorship committee member coordinating the training session should remind the mentors of the benefits of being at the training session. One benefit is that they will have their first 1:1 meeting with their mentee to begin goal setting and developing a work plan for the rest of the year.

Even more importantly, tell the mentors that the training session is where the group dynamic and sense of community starts to develop, and that you need them to be there. The relationships between the participants are critical to the success of the mentoring relationships each year, and every year your group dynamic will be different. Some mentorship groups are serious in their approach. Other years, the groups are more lighthearted. Some years the sense of community forms by the end of the training session. Other years, it takes much longer for the participants to think and act as a cohesive group.

Being at the training session to participate in this process is critical for the mentors. Their relationships with the newer mentorship program participants start to develop. It helps them expand their professional network. At the training session, they also have a chance to deepen their relationships with the mentors who are also returning to participate that year.

So, if a mentor asks if they really must attend the training session, either a mentorship committee member or the mentorship program leader should remind them it is a program requirement. There are many ways the mentorship program is structured around the mentors' personal and professional commitments. Attending the training session is one of the times it really doesn't work to accommodate the mentors' time considerations.

Logistics

Deciding Which Day – Our training sessions are on a Saturday morning, which requires the program participants to take time away from their family and personal lives to attend. Every year we ask the mentorship program participants to suggest a different time and day of the week to hold the training session. And every year they tell us Saturday morning is the only time they can devote enough time to be at this meeting.

Directions – If your training session is on a Saturday morning, you may have to find a different location if your usual meeting place is only available on weekdays. Make sure everyone receives and reads the directions to the training session. Every year at least one mentorship program participant arrives late because they didn't check the meeting request and went to the regular meeting location.

Traffic – It even helps if the committee member responsible for the training session monitors road blockages and construction scheduled for the day of your training session.

One year, on the same weekend as our training session, the main freeway in our area closed in both directions to install a new overpass! Fortunately, an alert member of the mentorship committee heard about the freeway closure in time to send out alternate directions to the meeting location.

Depending on your geography and the time of year, you may also want to monitor weather reports and have an alternate plan for conducting the training session in case of inclement weather. The lesson to be learned from these situations: every detail counts in planning your program meetings.

How Much Time? – A three-hour training session seems to be the best way to cover the theoretical basis of your mentorship program. Understanding there is a beginning, middle, and end to their approximately one-year mentoring relationship will give the participants a framework to understand the ebb and flow of their mentoring relationship throughout the year-long program. Scheduling the training session for two or three hours also allows the mentorship pairs enough time to begin planning the details of their mentoring relationship.

PowerPoint Presentation – The fundamental goal of the training session is to give the mentor-mentee pairs both the tools and the time to begin their work together. One of the tools offered with this book is a Microsoft PowerPoint presentation with information about mentorship and the mentor-mentee relationship. The mentorship program leader is responsible for preparing the PowerPoint presentation and leading the training session. We recommend doing it this way, since it is the most direct way to establish the mentorship program leader as the head of the program. The program leader is usually the most knowledgeable about the program. They were also probably instrumental in the chapter's decision to start a mentorship program.

Presentation Equipment – The mentorship committee member coordinating the training session needs to arrange for a laptop computer and a projector to display the training session presentation. Ask the facility ahead of time about the requirements and specifications for using a laptop in the training room. Coordinate with the facility manager to set up a time for a test run and make sure everything works ahead of time.

Handouts – There are quite a few documents to update and print for the training session. This includes the PowerPoint presentation slides and all the documents the mentor-mentee pairs will use during the training session. After the training session, the mentorship program leader can send the training documents in electronic format (PDF files) to each mentorship program participant who requests them.

Note: Appendix E: Training Session *provides a detailed list of the handouts and notes on how to use them. Links to the handouts available on the Internet are included in the Resources Download area.*

Start assembling the training session packets with the handouts and printed presentation slides at least a week before the training session.

Prepare one packet per participant and an additional leader's packet for the mentorship program leader.

On the day of the training session, have a presentation folder with the session agenda, presentation slides, and handouts printed and ready for all the participants.

The committee member chosen to plan and execute all the details for the training session can organize the printing of the handouts. The chapter should reimburse them for any printing costs. One way for the chapter to save money is to ask a local business to cover the cost of the printing. We've had sponsors pay for the cost of printing the packets. Some of our chapter sponsors did this as an "in-kind" donation, by printing the packets at their place of business.

Something you may want to consider in advance is the cost to the chapter and to the environment of printing a set of the presentation slides and all the handouts for the training session for each participant. To accommodate both these concerns, you can send the handouts in PDF attachments as part of the reminder email for the training session. And in the message, tell your participants the handouts will not be provided at the training session.

Before you decide to take this path, think about the age range of your participants. If your participants are reflective of most workplaces, there will be some Millennials in the group. It's very possible that some of them use their phone as their primary electronic device outside the workplace.

We found out the hard way that PDF documents aren't always noticeable when received on cellular phones. One year, we decided to be environmentally conscious and sent the training handouts as PDF documents attached to the reminder message for the training session. Two mentees came to the training session with no knowledge of any handouts. Their primary device for checking email was their phone, and they didn't see the attachments in the message. Needless to say, they weren't as prepared to participate in the training session as we had hoped.

If you decide to try sending the handouts in PDF format, tell the participants that the handouts are attached to the message, and ask that they read them before the training session. Add a request that they print and bring with them the handouts they want to use for reference or as part of their discussions with their mentor or mentee at the training session. Then, just for good measure, we suggest you also print a few copies of all the handouts to bring to the training session for participants who didn't see the attachments.

A lack of handouts for reference materials at the training is a disservice for your visual learners; they will have no way to remember the material from the presentation.

In addition, one of the group activities at the training session is a discussion between each of the mentor-mentee pairs about the ground rules for their relationship during the mentorship program. There is a handout for them to list these ground rules, called "key agreements," in the handouts for the training session. Without the printed materials to refer to, most participants find it hard to complete this or other group activities at the training session.

We also tried printing all the handouts but not the presentation slides, in an effort to save at least some of the environment. Predictably, there were complaints at the training session about the difficulty of understanding the presentation without the printed slides. They also weren't pleased about being unable to take notes on the handout with the printed presentation slides.

You may have decided by now that regardless of the cost to the chapter and the environment, providing printed materials at the training session is non-negotiable. We agree. Experience has shown that it is an expectation of the mentorship program participants for a copy of the printed materials to be provided at the training session.

Refreshments – One of the training session goals is to give the participants a chance to meet each other and begin networking. Serving food is a great way to help people relax in an unfamiliar setting. For that reason we suggest that your training session begin with food. If you choose to have the training session on a Saturday morning, a catered continental breakfast provided by the chapter is a nice touch. This also helps latecomers avoid the embarrassment of walking in late to the training session once it has begun.

As mentioned before, one way to save money for your chapter is to solicit volunteers at the mentor and mentees' pre-meetings to provide food and beverages for the training session. The mentorship committee member in charge of the training session needs to bring a separate refreshments sign-up sheet for the mentors and the mentees with the dates of the monthly meetings for each group. Before the end of the training session, a mentorship committee member should make sure all the participants have signed up to provide food or beverages for one of the monthly meetings.

Debrief – Because you probably rented a location for the training session, it is the responsibility of the mentorship committee to stay a few minutes after the end of the session to tidy up the room. Many public entities charge an additional fee if the room isn't left clean after an event. Asking the mentorship committee members to straighten the room after the training session prevents additional charges to the chapter.

The best reason to ask the mentorship committee to stay a few minutes after the meeting is completely unrelated to saving any additional charges for the chapter. After the training session, the mentorship committee members are energized from seeing the results of all their hard work come together at the training session. They usually have a need to discuss the results of the training session.

Immediately after the participants leave is a great time to do a quick check-in with the committee members and hear everyone's observations about what went well, what could be improved, and solicit new ideas to incorporate into the training session the following year. The cleaning up can be done during your debrief session. The time flies by, the room gets cleaned, and the mentorship committee has a chance to give themselves a well-deserved pat on the back.

Conducting the Training Session

Agenda

Time	Topic	Applicable Handout(s)
15 minutes	Refreshments	
1 hour	• Welcome, room logistics, and overview of objectives • Icebreaker introduction activity	• PowerPoint slides • Mentee-mentor matches list • Meeting topic list
10 minutes	Break	

Time	Topic	Applicable Handout(s)
10 minutes	Phase One – Preparing • Emphasize the preparation work has been done • Explain the participants have been in the preparing stage since submitting their applications to the program	• Strategies and Considerations for Initial Conversations • Mentoring Pre-Work • Engaging the Mentee • Roles, Responsibilities of Effective Mentors and Mentees • Reasonable Expectations for Mentors and Mentees
30 minutes	Phase Two – Negotiating • Activity: Mentor-mentee pairs meet individually to begin discussing their goals for the program	• Personal Inventory Tool • Career and Life Goals • Setting Goals • Development Activities for Mentees • Identifying Learning Opportunities • Generating a List of Learning Opportunities • Developing the Work Plan • Setting Relationship Parameters • Mentoring Partnership Agreement • Partnership Agreement Template • Streamlined Mentoring Partnership Agreement Template • Readiness Checklist • Negotiating Questions and Outcomes
15 minutes	Break	
20 minutes	Phase Three – Enabling • Activity: Mentor-mentee pairs meet individually to discuss ground rules for their relationship	• Mentoring Builds Great Leaders, But Only If There Is Fierce Honesty • Assessing the Partnership • Listening and Feedback Skills • Strategies for Overcoming Obstacles

Time	Topic	Applicable Handout(s)
10 minutes	Phase Four – Closing • Activity: Mentor-mentee pairs meet individually to begin discussing possible signs of early closure	• Signals That It Might Be Time For Closure • Closure Preparation: Steps and Questions • Closing: A Readiness Checklist • Turning Closure Into Learning
5 minutes	Support for the Process • Identify and begin developing the networks and chapter support available for the mentorship pairs	
15 minutes	Next Steps • Activity: Mentor-mentee pairs meet individually to identify and plan their next steps	
10-20 minutes	Closing Remarks • Reinforce next group meeting(s) date, time, and location • Questions from participants	• Pass out individual gift cards

Note: *This agenda is included in* Appendix E: Training Session *and can be downloaded from the Resources Download area.*

Training Session Presentation

Introductions – We begin the training session with introductions in the form of a group exercise. This helps all the participants get to know each other beyond the time available to talk at the speed mentoring session. You can use any icebreaker that you find works as a group exercise.

During the icebreaker, we suggest you ask each participant to answer several questions about themselves. The questions are related to personal information they would feel comfortable sharing in a group. It helps if you write the questions on a whiteboard, or on a large display pad with permanent marker, and hang the paper on the wall.

The following are some other sample questions for your group activity:

• Where did you grow up?

• How many siblings (if any) are in your family?

• What is the birth order in your family?

• What do you do to have fun?

- Tell us about your first job, your first career goal, or your favorite activity as a child.

Allow 45 minutes for this activity, depending on the number of participants in your mentorship program. Plan for less time if there are less than 8 mentor-mentee pairs in your mentorship program. This process will take a full hour if you have 12 – 15 mentor-mentee pairs in your mentorship program.

The Mentoring Relationship – The remainder of the training session is divided between the information in the PowerPoint presentation and the activities of the mentor-mentee pairs. The presentation and the activities are designed to help the mentor-mentee pairs set their goals and objectives for the program and start negotiating their relationship, including key agreements such as when and where they plan to meet each month.

One outcome of the training session is for the mentorship pairs to start work on their plan to achieve their goals. They mutually agree on a working contract and determine how they will measure their success at the end of the program.

Dedicate time at the training session for the mentor-mentee pairs to discuss how to support each other during their mentoring relationship. In both the presentation and the leader's remarks, you should make an important point about the need for each participant to be committed to complete communication within their mentoring relationship. By listening to each other, and giving and receiving feedback, the participants are more likely to succeed in achieving their goals for the program.

Choosing A New Path – The training session presentation slides reference Robert Frost's poem, "The Road Not Taken." This is included to emphasize that by being a part of your mentorship program, the participants have chosen a different path for their lives than the one they were on before they applied. They are embarking on a journey, and the training session is designed to start them off on their new path with as much information and support as possible.

One thing we discovered is that when people decide to make a change, other areas of their lives change also. It is almost as though making the decision to change the course of their professional lives has a ripple effect into the other areas of their lives. In the course of just one year, we have seen participants marry and divorce, change jobs, and change careers. Many participants move locally and a few may relocate to other states during the mentorship program. Participants may become pregnant. Occasionally someone becomes too ill to participate or sadly, passes away during the course of the mentorship program. You will need to expect the unexpected, and support your mentorship participants to the best of your ability on their journey.

Closing – Near the end of the training session, we talk about the last phase of the mentoring relationship: closing. The end of the program is one obvious way the mentor-mentees experience closure for this very important relationship.

However, in the course of a year many unforeseen events can occur. Try to prepare your mentorship program participants from the very beginning that despite their best intentions, things may not go as they plan. Because change seems to be a major factor for mentorship program participants, the training session includes information on what to do if one or both people in the mentor-mentee pair need to leave the program.

We suggest you include this information to prepare your participants for the ups and down they may encounter on this journey. Offer suggestions on what to do if it becomes clear their mentoring relationship is ending, intentional or not. It's also important to make sure that if it does end, they know how to get support from the mentorship committee members.

Post-Training Follow Up

After the training session is over, the room is cleaned, and your committee has debriefed, it's important to follow up with the mentorship program participants about their next steps and the date, time, and location of the next mentorship program meeting. There is a sense among both the mentorship committee members and the participants that they have completed a milestone. That is true, but the road continues. It's important to start everyone thinking about the rest of the journey as soon as possible.

During the training session, some of the mentors and mentees usually request copies of the handouts in PDF format. The follow up message is a good time to send all the handouts from the training session in electronic format to all the participants.

As we mentioned, sending these documents before the training session is not beneficial, and in fact detracts from the effectiveness of the training session. No later than the day after the training session, the committee member who coordinated the event should send an email to all the participants with the following:

- Training session handouts
- Confirmation of the next program meeting(s), including date, time, and location

Training Session Summary

Training Session Activities

Step #	Process	Description	Person Assigned
Step 1	Prepare		
	Communicate training session information	• Send message to participants with logistics of the training session	Committee member
	Arrange for refreshments	• Coordinate food, beverages, and utensils	Committee member
	Organize the training session	• Prepare laptop for presentation use	Program leader or designated presenter

Step #	Process	Description	Person Assigned
		• Print and collate individuals packets with handouts	Committee member
Step 2	Conduct the training session		Program leader
Step 3	Post-training follow up		Committee member
		Send email to all participants with:	
		Training session handouts	
		Confirmation of the next program meeting(s), including date, time, and location	

Training Session Roles and Responsibilities

Role	Responsibility
Mentorship program leader	• Select committee member to coordinate training session preparations • Prepare PowerPoint presentation • Lead training session
Mentorship committee member	• Communications about training session • Prepare training materials • Arrange for refreshments
Mentors and mentees	• Attend training session and participate fully

Chapter 7
MONTHLY PROGRAM MEETINGS

Participants see the training session as the "real" beginning of the mentorship program. Then, within a week or two of the training session, the monthly group meetings begin and the mentor-mentee pairs start working together to accomplish the mentee's developmental goals.

The purpose of this chapter is to provide guidelines and information about how to ensure your monthly group meetings help the mentorship program participants achieve their goals for the program. In the chapter on goal setting and planning, we discussed logistics planning for the various mentorship program meetings. Now it's time to go into much more depth on the details of the monthly program meetings.

This chapter walks you through the process of arranging and facilitating these monthly meetings, and monitoring the participants' progress.

Monthly Meetings

Within two weeks after the training session, both the mentorship groups and the mentor-mentee pairs start meeting monthly.

One way for the mentorship committee to coordinate the monthly meetings is to divide the work between conducting the monthly meetings, and tracking participation of the mentorship participants.

If your mentorship program has three to five mentorship pairs, one person can probably handle everything involved in conducting the monthly meetings and tracking the participants' participation.

If your mentorship program has more than five mentor-mentee pairs, it's a good idea for two different committee members to take on these responsibilities. One committee member should be in charge of making sure the monthly meetings happen on time and as planned. Another committee member should track attendance at the monthly meetings as well as collect and collate the progress reports from the participants every month.

Together or Separate?

We suggest you start the monthly program meetings with all the mentorship program participants meeting as a combined group the first month. Then the following month, the mentors and mentees should meet separately in their groups.

For the remainder of the mentorship program, continue that same pattern of mentors and mentees meeting as a combined group one month and separately the following month.

An easy way to remember the pattern is to use the idea of scheduling the combined group meetings in the odd-numbered months (March, May, July, and September) and the separate group meetings in the even-numbered months. If you decide to do it this way, your program meeting schedule would look like this:

Month	Week Day	Meeting Description
March	First Saturday	Training session
	Third Tuesday	Mentor and mentee combined meeting
April	Second Monday	Mentee group meeting
	Second Tuesday	Mentor group meeting
May	Second Tuesday	Mentor and mentee combined meeting
June	Second Monday	Mentee group meeting
	Second Tuesday	Mentor group meeting
July	Second Tuesday	Mentor and mentee combined meeting
August	Second Monday	Mentee group meeting
	Second Tuesday	Mentor group meeting

Month	Week Day	Meeting Description
September	Second Tuesday	Mentor and mentee combined meeting
October	Second Monday	Mentee group meeting
	Second Tuesday	Mentor group meeting
November	Second Tuesday	Mentor and mentee combined meeting

The following is an example of a handout with the mentorship program meeting dates, based on the above sequence.

Note: This handout is included in Appendix F: Monthly Program Meetings

<CHAPTER NAME> MENTORSHIP PROGRAM
20XX MEETINGS

Mentees	Mentors
Tuesday, February 28, 20XX – Mentee Pre-Meeting	Tuesday, February 21, 20XX – Mentor Pre-Meeting
Tuesday, March 6, 20XX – Speed Mentoring	Tuesday, March 6, 20XX – Speed Mentoring
Saturday, March 17, 20XX – Training Session	Saturday, March 17, 20XX – Training Session
Tuesday, March 20, 20XX – Combined Meeting	Tuesday, March 20, 20XX – Combined Meeting
Monday, April 16, 20XX – Mentees Meeting	Tuesday, April 17, 20XX – Mentors Meeting
Tuesday, May 15, 20XX – Combined Meeting	Tuesday, May 15, 20XX – Combined Meeting
Monday, June 11, 20XX – Mentees Meeting	Tuesday, June 12, 20XX – Mentors Meeting
Tuesday, July 10, 20XX – Combined Meeting	Tuesday, July 10, 20XX – Combined Meeting
Monday, August 13, 20XX – Mentees Meeting	Tuesday, August 14, 20XX – Mentors Meeting
Tuesday, September 11, 20XX – Combined Meeting	Tuesday, September 11, 20XX – Combined Meeting
Monday, October 15, 20XX – Mentees Meeting	Tuesday, October 16, 20XX – Mentors Meeting
Tuesday, November 6, 20XX – Combined Meeting	Tuesday, November 6, 20XX – Combined Meeting
Thursday, November 8, 20XX Chapter Meeting 11:30 AM – 1:00 PM <Meeting Location> <Location Address>	Thursday, November 8, 20XX Chapter Meeting 11:30 AM – 1:00 PM <Meeting Location> <Location Address>

MEETING LOCATION:

All meetings except the Training Session will be held at:
<Meeting Location>
<Location Address>

MEETING TIMES:

Training Session: 9 AM – 12 Noon
Monthly Meetings: 6 PM – 8 PM
November Chapter Meeting: 11:30 AM – 1 PM

Prepare this list of meeting dates during the planning process for your mentorship program. It is crucial to the planning process to know exactly when and how often the groups will be meeting.

We recommend telling the participants early and often just how many meetings they will be required to attend as part of the mentorship program. That's why this list is one of the handouts for the mentor and mentees' pre-meetings.

Location of Monthly Meetings

Hopefully, the question of where to hold your monthly meetings was decided during the planning process. As mentioned in the planning chapter, arranging the location for the monthly meetings is a huge task, and very time-consuming.

If a consistent location for the monthly group meetings hasn't been arranged, designate a committee member whose sole responsibility for the remainder of the program is to arrange the venue, communicate the meeting location information to all of the mentorship program participants each month, and follow-up on attendance.

Knowing the meeting location each month is crucial for the participants in planning their program participation. A mentorship committee member must send the location information and directions to the participants at least a week in advance of the monthly group meeting(s).

For the purposes of this chapter, we assume the mentorship committee arranged your meeting location during the planning phase, and the meeting location information was communicated to the mentorship program participants before the mentorship program started.

Refreshments

One way to have your mentorship participants "own" their participation in the program is to ask them to provide refreshments for the monthly group meetings. When the program participants coordinate who is bringing beverages and who is bringing food, they have an opportunity to develop a relationship with someone else in the program other than their mentor or mentee. Having them provide refreshments is a simple and not-so-subtle method of encouraging the mentorship program participants to get to know each other better.

Asking the participants to provide the meeting refreshments also saves the chapter money. Depending on the number of mentorship program participants, this is a significant savings for the chapter. It may be the deciding factor whether you can afford to start a mentorship program.

For both these reasons, we suggest you ask the mentorship program participants to bring refreshments for their monthly group meetings. It becomes a very smooth process after the first round of group meetings: They sign up in advance at the training session, and one of the mentorship committee members reminds them about a week in advance that they volunteered to bring the refreshments for the group meeting that month.

Conducting the Monthly Meetings

The steps involved in conducting the monthly group meetings aren't complicated, but each step must be done every month for your meetings to be successful.

There are a number of small details that are part of preparing for and conducting each group meeting. Ask a mentorship committee member who excels at planning to take over the monthly meeting details. The timing of the process leading up to each monthly meeting is also crucial. Below is a list of the steps to be completed every month, including the timing for each step.

Two weeks before the meeting:

- Confirm date, time, and room location with facility

One week before the meeting:

- Confirm presenter attendance and ask about requirements for presentation (equipment, etc.)

- Arrange technical equipment and/or printing of handouts (as needed)

- Update calendar meeting request with meeting topic, name of presenter, and location (as needed)

- Re-send calendar meeting request to all participants, including presenter(s)

- Send any documents related to presentation to all participants in electronic format

- Monitor meeting acceptances from updated meeting request

- Remind participants who signed up to bring refreshments, tell them the number of expected attendees, and ask them to arrive 15 minutes early

Day of the meeting:

- Bring paper goods (napkins, paper plates, plastic cutlery, cups, etc.) to meeting

- Remind participants to sign attendance list as they arrive

- Assist participants with setting up refreshments before the meeting

- Assist participants with cleaning up refreshments after the meeting

Day after the meeting:

- Send follow-up documents related to meeting topic

Meeting Notifications

As technology has evolved over the last few years, a variety of ways have surfaced to notify participants about the monthly group meetings. Unfortunately, no one method works for everyone. Here is a list of the tools available, and the pros and cons of each one:

Email – allows you to send a note to the participants each month, reminding them of the monthly meeting location, date, and time. Everyone uses email in some format, but the main drawback is the participants also have to add the meeting to their own calendar. If they don't, meeting attendance suffers. It will become clear soon after the first meeting or two if asking your participants to add the meetings to their calendars is effective.

Evite® – this is very useful for reminding participants of the monthly meetings. It also allows you to somewhat track who plans to attend.

Unfortunately, sometimes these invitations end up in spam filters.

You may also have a certain percentage of participants who see the message but just don't respond. That complicates planning for refreshments, since you will never know exactly who will attend. It also creates a lot of work for the mentorship committee member tracking attendance.

To be certain of who is attending, the mentorship committee must call all the participants who don't respond. Sometimes it takes multiple calls and messages, only to find out the person planned to be there all along. If they didn't see the invitation or it was in their spam folder, by then it's difficult for the mentorship committee member to get them to re-arrange their schedule to be at the meeting in a few days.

Meeting Requests – allows you to schedule the monthly group meetings on every participant's calendar. The format we suggest and have used the most is **meeting requests.** They greatly improve attendance by allowing the mentorship committee member to easily track responses and follow up via telephone with those who don't respond in a timely way.

This method isn't fool-proof. Sometimes participants using different software for their personal email and calendar provider have trouble sending, receiving, or responding to meeting requests. Even so, using meeting requests to reserve time on participants' calendars will still give you the best attendance at the monthly group meetings. This is by far the preferred method of participants to help them remember and attend the monthly group meetings.

Alternating the combined group meetings with separate mentor and mentee group meetings means the mentees meet on Mondays some months and on Tuesdays the other months. As this varying schedule can create scheduling confusion for some people, the monthly meeting date must be confirmed prior to each group meeting.

Scheduling Meetings for the Mentorship Program

Because the mentorship committee determined the meeting dates and scheduled the group meetings during the planning phase, you can send meeting requests to the participants for all the monthly meetings immediately after the training session.

Tell the participants at the training session they should expect to receive meeting requests for the entire mentorship program within a few days. Let them know who will be sending the requests so they can look for and locate them. If the meeting invitations are blocked by a spam filter, the participant should mark them as "safe" once they are located.

Then, for the remainder of the mentorship program the participant should review the meetings requests each month before the group meeting. You should also set the expectation that everyone needs to respond to each meeting request when it arrives.

Current Contact Information

Many of your participants may prefer to use their work email address while participating in the mentorship program. However, if they change jobs during the program, they lose the meeting dates, times, and location for the rest of the mentorship program. For that reason, ask them to use their home email address, or both their home and work email addresses, for all their mentorship program communications. You should also tell them early, and remind them often, to tell the mentorship committee as soon as they start a new job.

Notifying the mentorship committee about their new job may sound like a small thing, but you can expect about 20% – 25% of your mentorship program participants to change jobs during the mentorship program. For that reason, we recommend that one mentorship committee member should "own" the task of keeping the participant contact list up to date. This includes sending updated contact information to the rest of the participants.

The participants appreciate the time and energy spent by the mentorship committee keeping everyone's contact information up to date for two reasons:

1. Everyone knows how to reach each other if a question comes up about their area of interest or expertise

2. Keeping everyone's contact information current gives participants a chance to congratulate each other about a new job or other special event.

Tracking Monthly Attendance and Progress

The committee member responsible for tracking monthly meeting attendance and progress forms monitors the participation of each mentorship program participant. Perhaps even more than the mentorship program leader, they are the most likely to notice a pattern of non-participation by a mentee or mentor.

This committee member literally has their finger on the pulse of the mentorship program. It follows that you want to choose the committee member who does this follow up carefully. Look for these traits:

- **Observation and follow-up skills:** these skills are crucial in detecting and intervening in attendance issues and problems with the relationship between mentor-mentee pairs.

- **Experienced listener:** they must identify when a problem surfaces and involve the rest of the mentorship committee and/or participants if needed.

- **Problem solver:** having experience in "crucial conversations" is critical for this role on the mentorship committee

It may sound like overkill to track group meeting attendance. Experience has repeatedly shown that participants who miss group meetings are most at risk of dropping out of the mentorship program. There are a variety of reasons why someone might miss group meetings, but the end result is the same.

Following up with a participant who misses a group meeting helps you discover if there are problems with their mentoring relationship, or work or family issues, in time to help solve the problem.

Not following up allows the situation to go on until the only solution is that they quit the mentorship program early.

The best time for follow up about a missed group meeting is the day after the scheduled meeting. The committee member should compare the sign-in list for that meeting with names of the participants expected. You can start the follow up process with an email. But, if the participant doesn't reply the initial email within 24 – 48 hours, it's important that the next step is for you to call them directly.

It should come as no surprise to a participant if a mentorship committee member contacts them when they miss a mentorship program meeting. You will find that when the mentorship committee member is diligent about contacting participants who miss meetings, attendance at the meeting is much higher.

In fact, since the participant knows they will be contacted, sometimes they send their regrets before anyone needs to call or email them. This also saves time for the mentorship committee member, which is always appreciated.

Critical Role of a Committee

The role of the mentorship committee members cannot be overstated. The first few years, our mentorship "committee" consisted of only one person. They had a hard time doing everything suggested in this book with 20+ mentorship program participants.

Then we added mentorship committee members, with great results. There were more people available to follow up with attendance and relationship issues, and they had time to intervene earlier when problems came up.

Immediately, we saw a higher percentage of mentorship program participants completing the program. We recommend beginning your mentorship program with at least two or three people on the mentorship committee, with their specific goal being to have enough time to follow up quickly with participants.

Life Happens

The reasons mentorship program participants miss meetings are as individual as each participant. Every year, you will have participants who review the list of meeting dates at the beginning of the program and notify the mentorship committee of any absences, such as a planned vacation. The mentorship committee member in charge of attendance should make note of these absences to save themselves time and effort later in the program.

Unfortunately, no one has a completely predictable schedule. Many participants have travel related to work that isn't scheduled in advance. Everyone has the possibility of family emergencies or personal illness that happens on or around the date of a scheduled monthly meeting.

If a participant tells you in advance they need to be absent for a group meeting, note the reasons for these absences at the time they are communicated. Then, they can be excused when the meeting date arrives. In addition, it's a nice touch make sure the participant receives any meeting handouts or presentation slides from that meeting to help them feel they are still included.

The Bigger Issue

Sometimes a participant decides not to attend group meetings because they are dissatisfied with the mentorship program or their mentor or mentee. If you suspect this is happening, following up about a missed group meeting gives the participant a chance to vent, either on the phone or in person with the mentorship committee member.

There are many, many reasons why a participant might be dissatisfied with the mentorship program. Even with all the communication before the start of the program, they may be resentful of the time commitment. It may help to involve their mentor or mentee to negotiate shorter or less frequent 1:1 meetings if the time involved in the program is the issue.

Hearing a participant bring up dissatisfaction with their mentor or mentee is a big concern for the mentorship committee. It nearly always involves a miscommunication or unrealistic expectation between the mentor and mentee. In this situation, the mentorship committee can encourage them to meet to discuss the problem.

Sometimes it helps if as member skilled in difficult conversations meets with the mentor and mentee to resolve things. In these cases, it helps a great deal if the mentor is willing to lead the discussion. Frequently, the mentor is familiar with this role from their work experience in HR. In these cases, it is usually possible for the mentor-mentee pair to work through the conflict, and the mentor-mentee bond is strengthened as part of the process.

Of course, cooperation is required on both sides to resolve disagreements between members of a mentor-mentee pair. Sometimes by the time it is brought up to the mentorship committee, the dissatisfied person is no longer willing to continue in the program.

Frequently the problem is not the mentor-mentee relationship. If a participant indicates they may quit the mentorship program, it's important to try to find out why, and if possible help them stay the course. This is why you need someone skilled in difficult conversations in this committee member role. They need to know what they can do and what to promise in working with the participant.

Just as importantly, the mentorship committee member needs to know what might be considered unreasonable requests on the part of the participant. Usually, these situations aren't discussed in advance. With the mentorship committee and participants depending on them, the committee member may feel the need to go above and beyond to keep the participant in the program. We suggest that they don't.

Doing more or making additional promises to keep a participant in the mentorship program may work in the short term. We have found that in these instances the special treatment becomes an expectation, and the additional requests continue and escalate until the participant leaves the program early, despite everything done on their behalf.

In these situations, the mentorship committee member should use their judgment about whether the problem can be resolved. They also need to know they have the support of the mentorship committee and the program leader, regardless of the outcome of the discussion.

Sometimes all the concern, discussion, meetings and interventions available don't make a difference. Sometimes you hear about the problem long after the event, and the participant's mind is made up that they need to quit the mentorship program. As mentioned before, occasionally you may not find out about their dissatisfaction until the participant has literally moved on.

It's always a good idea to try to resolve the issues that come up. Communicating about the problem isn't a miracle cure; it doesn't always help solve the problem. However, in these cases we've found that no follow up is always ineffective and leads to participants leaving the mentorship program before the scheduled completion date.

Monthly Meeting Topics

Knowing the monthly meeting topic in advance benefits the mentorship program participants. Mentees appreciate knowing what areas of their professional development are on the agenda for that month's meeting. Mentors have a variety of reasons for wanting to know in advance the discussion topics for the mentees.

Mentors may also have an interest in a specific topic and decide to attend the mentees' group meeting in addition to their own group meeting the following night. In addition, it allows them to focus on alternate topics during their 1:1 meetings with their mentee. It also helps them plan the professional development activities they will be focusing on with their mentee throughout the program.

Mentee Group Meeting Topics

After quite a bit of experimentation with different meeting formats and feedback from the mentees, we've found that mentees prefer their monthly group meetings to be structured. They like hearing about a topic related to human resource management or professional development.

Feel free to invite guest speakers with expertise on these topics to your mentee group meetings. If you decide to start with 10 or more mentor-mentee pairs, you will have at least three or four mentors who are subject matter experts on topics you want to include in the mentees' group meetings. Even if yours is a small chapter, it is very likely that some members are experts in one or more areas of professional development.

It's important to note here that we are not suggesting the mentees' group meeting topics be related to HR specialties, such as labor relations or compensation. Some of the mentees won't be interested in spending two hours discussing the finer points of creating a compensation plan.

Even if one or more of the mentorship committee members is an expert in one of these areas, focusing on an HR specialty area for an entire group meeting is not the point of the mentorship program.

Instead, the mentees' group meeting topics should be of interest to all the mentees, regardless of specialty or expertise.

Personal Branding and Networking – The most positive feedback from the mentees in our program has been about our networking and personal branding presentations. Several of our mentors developed these presentations specifically for our mentorship program. They are always rated highly by the mentees as being very applicable to achieving their goals for the mentorship program.

LinkedIn – A perennial mentee favorite is a presentation on making the most of their LinkedIn profile. Every year several of our mentees list as one of their goals finding their next level job in HR. Since LinkedIn is a worldwide tool used for professional networking and recruiting, it helps them to learn how to present themselves professionally. A presentation about using LinkedIn will be invaluable to your participants in their search for new positions.

You may want to schedule this presentation during a mentee group meeting, and invite the mentors to attend. That approach seems to work best: include just the people who are interested. We predict this presentation will become a standard for your mentorship program.

Professional Development Topics – A popular meeting topic related to professional development is a presentation on the Myers-Briggs Type Indicator® (MBTI) test. You may have a chapter member who specializes in this area of HR. If so, they may be able to come and administer the MBTI to the mentees and discuss their results as part of a presentation on understanding the usefulness of the MBTI in developing successful working relationships.

HR Case Studies – A very popular topics is a monthly group meeting with a discussion of HR case studies. Because the mentorship committee and the mentors are all experienced HR professionals, you probably have an abundance of case studies to use for this presentation. Your mentees will be sure to rate the HR case studies presentation as one of their top three favorites for the group meetings.

There are multiple ways to present HR case studies. You can schedule it for a mentee group meeting and the mentees must choose the important legal implications for HR in each case study. You can also schedule it as the topic of a combined group meeting, with both the mentees and mentors. Doing it this way is very popular, because the mentors enjoy helping the presenter by suggesting legal issues to consider in each case study.

One reason to try different presentations for the HR case studies is that the experience level of the mentees in your mentorship program will vary from year to year. This creates a unique challenge for the presenter in facilitating the case studies discussion.

Some years, the average HR experience of the mentees may be closer to mid-level than emerging HR professionals. When that happens, the mentees arrive at their conclusions about a case study after only a few minutes of discussion. Then even with three or four case studies to discuss the meeting is over much earlier than planned.

Other years, the majority of the mentees might be transitioning to HR from other professions. The case study presentation is much more challenging those years. Mentees with less HR experience have trouble determining the important legal concepts in the case studies. This requires the presenter to be far more direct during the discussion to help the group reach a conclusion about the case study. Both experience levels have their challenges. We have found the best way to help the case studies presenter prepare is to inform them in advance about the HR experience level of the mentee group.

"President's Perspective" – Another meeting topic consistently rated high by our mentees is inviting the current chapter president to attend the final mentee group meeting to talk about the "President's Perspective." By that time in the program, the mentees have achieved many of their goals for professional development set earlier in the year. With the end of the mentorship program approaching, most of them are already pondering the next step in their career.

We suggest that your current chapter president start the presentation with an informal discussion about their own career in human resource management, with time included for the mentees to ask questions. The mentees find it inspiring to hear a chapter leader talk about their career in human resource management. This is important for your mentees: The mentees may have never met or spoken with the chapter president and they will really appreciate this opportunity.

The mentees' experience in the mentorship program always strengthens their commitment to the chapter. Many of them will express a desire to "give back" to the chapter when the mentorship program is over. We found that encouraging them to become a chapter volunteer is the perfect way for them to accomplish that goal. So, try building that topic into the president's discussion. About an hour into the meeting, ask the president to steer the conversation towards volunteer opportunities within the chapter.

As a follow-up to the mentorship program, volunteering on a committee is a great way for mentees to continue their professional development. It gives them another opportunity to expand their professional network. Another benefit in volunteering is the chance for the committee chair to notice them as a future chapter leader. Many mentees see value for themselves in this path. They frequently seize the opportunity, sometimes before the mentorship program is even over.

Before starting the mentorship program, we struggled with succession planning for the chapter leadership. With a group of early to mid-career chapter members completing the mentorship program each year, and with many of them becoming chapter volunteers, we find this is no longer an issue. There is a natural progression from mentee to committee volunteer to committee leader, to board of directors volunteer, to the chapter executive board. Adding the President's Perspective as the last mentee group meeting of each year has helped to create this succession path and strengthened the chapter.

Mentor Group Meeting Topics

One of the most precious commodities for your mentors is time. Added to that is the travel time mentors must invest to participate in the mentorship program. Every year, key feedback from our mentors is that they want to make sure the time they spend in the monthly group meetings is valuable. So, try to make the most of their time by involving them in activities that add value for their mentees.

Mentor Check-in – Part of each mentor group meeting should be a round robin check-in by all the mentors about the mentoring relationship with their mentee. This allows mentors a chance to share their experiences with each other and exchange ideas for addressing potential problems. It also alerts mentorship committee members and the program leader to the need for intervention. The feedback from mentors about the value of this exercise in their meetings will depend significantly on the quality of the relationships within the mentor group, in addition to other factors.

Not every mentor views the check-ins as a valuable way to spend mentor group time. To increase the usefulness of the process, try asking mentors to limit their comments to a green-yellow-red assessment of how things are going with their mentee, with up to 60 seconds of commentary on their assessment.

The first year we tried this method, compliance with the time limit varied significantly among the mentors. Some mentors were natural story tellers and took longer than their allotted time. And of course, the element of drama in certain situations must occasionally be part of the story. Other mentors had significant problems with their mentees, and needed more than one minute to describe their experience and assessment of the problem.

After trying this method, you will notice something significant. The number of questions asked and subsequent discussion about an individual mentor's assessment directly correlate to the value each mentor receives from the group process. Paying attention to the number of questions asked about an individual mentor's assessment will allow you to easily facilitate the discussion, and maximize the value of the process for all mentors. The number of questions asked is the essential ingredient that makes this process valuable for the mentors.

The round robin process usually takes up to an hour during each mentor group meeting. Since a combined group meeting is always scheduled the following month, the rest of each mentor group meeting should be devoted to preparing the mentors for their responsibility in the next month's combined group meeting. This will probably only take an hour, so the mentors know they will be able to leave on time. Many times the planning takes less than 30 minutes, and the mentors are always happy when their meeting ends early.

Combined Group Meeting Topics

The topics for each of the combined group meetings are chosen during the planning process. However, you never know when you will come across the next good idea for a meeting topic.

To get the best topics each year, be flexible and encourage the participants to make suggestions.

Why Not Act It Out? – Sometimes a mentorship participant has an idea for improving the mentorship program that changes everything. This happened one year with our HR case studies discussion. One of the mentors suggested acting out the HR case studies during a combined group meeting, with the mentors as the actors. The novelty of this suggestion intrigued the mentors, and most of them volunteered to be actors.

The mentor actors chose their own HR legal topic and teamed up based on their topic of choice. The legal issues selected were an EEOC audit, a discrimination case, and an unlawful dismissal case. They were given one month to work together to prepare their presentation, although two of the mentor pairs met just prior to the meeting to plan for their topic. Because they were using their own experience, it was easy for them to ad-lib and embellish their scenario as their presentation unfolded. One pair of mentors arrived in costume for their presentation, and stayed in character throughout the entire meeting.

To say this was the most successful case study presentation in our mentorship program would be a huge understatement. Adding the element of acting out the case studies fully engaged both the visual and the audio learners. The ensuing discussion about each case study was lively. Mentees with less HR experience had the opportunity to see the results of unlawful workplace activity and had no trouble understanding the legal points raised by each case study. Mentees closer to the mid-career level loved seeing the finer points of the law acted out with no risk of making an incorrect decision. By the end of the presentation, it was a foregone conclusion we would continue doing it the same way every year. Since that time, the case study presentation is always everyone's favorite group meeting in the mentorship program.

Informational Interviews – Informational interviews are of enormous value for individuals in all organizations and industries. Human resource management professionals recognize this, and we actively encourage the practice at all levels of the profession.

The first year of our mentorship program, the program leader and the mentors spent quite a bit of time encouraging mentees to use informational interviews to find out more about HR career paths and the organizations they were targeting in their career development. Mentees applying this advice found it helpful, and the positive results encouraged them to do more interviews.

You may notice that mentees doing informational interviews are more satisfied with their professional development in the mentorship program. They are also more likely to reach their goals for the program. We've found that the mentees most likely to participate in informational interviews consider themselves extroverts.

Several mentees who self-identify as introverts told us that asking a stranger for an appointment to do an informational interview was too far outside their comfort zone to consider. Armed with that feedback, we found a way to help every mentee experience the value of an informational interview in a safe setting.

By the middle of the mentorship program, the mentees have met all of the mentors at least once or twice: in the speed mentoring, the training session, and a combined group meeting. So, we suggest that you try scheduling informational interviews as the topic for one of the combined group meetings. Hopefully your more introverted mentees will find that a combined group meeting is a safe setting.

One of the easiest ways to include everyone in these informational interviews is to schedule three 20-minute informational interviews, with a five-minute break between each interview.

Once the informational interviews are completed, bring the entire group together during the remaining 45 minutes of that meeting for their feedback on the experience. The mentorship program leader should be in charge of timing each interview period and the breaks. The mentorship committee is in charge of making sure everyone takes a break and switches when they are supposed to.

To prepare the participants for this new idea, spend time in the preceding mentee and mentor group meetings preparing each group for their part in the informational interviews. Included in the download area are several Internet articles on how to do informational interviews. You can send these to all the participants as part of their preparation for this group meeting. You should also tell the mentees to update their résumés by the following month, and to bring three copies with them to the next meeting.

We recommend against having the participants choose their interview partner for each informational interview, even with the caveat that they may not choose their own mentor or mentee. The process of choosing who to speak with becomes overwhelming for some of the participants. If you try it this way, have the mentorship program leader ready to step in and help them find someone to interview before each interview round.

Although everyone eventually will eventually find a person to interview each time, the meeting room will become complete chaos for a few minutes with each interview switch. It also puts the less-outgoing mentees at a disadvantage because of the noise and the need to ask someone to talk to them. The feedback from doing it this way will probably be that the participants love the idea but found the noise and chaos difficult to accommodate. The interview pairs should spread out into adjoining rooms, but even that probably won't reduce the noise enough for people to hear each other.

If the first doesn't work for you, try this: create an interview schedule prior to the informational interview meeting. It will be easier for the participants to follow a list of people they are scheduled to interview. It will avoid having any of the participants interview their own mentor or mentee. Send the interview schedule to all of the mentorship program participants in advance of the meeting to give them time before arriving to research the people they will be interviewing. You should also try to schedule a bigger room for that meeting to help with the noise levels.

We've found that this process is much smoother, more orderly, and the noise level is lower. Even better, all the mentees said they felt more confident using the experience to begin setting up and completing their own informational interviews. We recommend using this process.

Hopefully you will notice a definite increase in the number of informational interviews completed by your mentees outside the program. Best of all, the mentees will receive a lot of value from their independently scheduled interviews after this process.

If you decide to use this topic and format, the best time to schedule the informational interviews is at a combined group meeting after the HR case study presentation. By waiting until then, the more reserved mentees are less nervous around all the mentors after seeing them in a more informal setting acting out the HR case studies.

Other Meeting Topics

If you need additional meeting topics, try to select them during the planning process. Then, be open to changing the schedule if someone has an idea for a new topic. Every one of the topics or processes that have become such a valuable addition to our mentorship program started as someone's great idea. Start out with a plan for your program and monthly meeting topics, and then encourage your mentorship committee to try something new when the opportunity arises.

For other combined meeting topics, we tried finding presenters on issues unrelated to professional development.

Some of the topics we tried were diversity and inclusion, generational differences, and global HR. They were popular topics, but we couldn't always be sure we were able to get a speaker back the following year. The feedback on these topics always had more to do with the quality of the speaker than the relevance of the topic to a career in human resource management. For these reasons, we suggest including the less specialized meeting topics mentioned previously.

Monitoring the Mentor-Mentee Pairs

Once you notify the mentor-mentee pairs of their match, they need to take responsibility to begin meeting one-on-one each month.

Ideally, every mentor-mentee pair will have an opportunity to meet before the first monthly group meeting.

To ensure the mentorship committee is informed on the progress and effectiveness of each mentor-mentee pair, we have both the mentor and the mentee complete and return a monthly progress form. The purpose of the monthly progress forms is to track the effectiveness of the mentoring relationship for each person in the mentor-mentee pairs.

Monthly Progress Forms

We suggest that you ask all your mentorship participants to complete a progress form every month to encourage them to reflect and report, from their own perspective, on the effectiveness of their mentoring relationship.

We found that the individual progress forms from mentor-mentee pairs whose relationship is effective and who are meeting their goals are remarkably similar in tone and the information reported about their progress is positive. See *Appendix F: Monthly Program Meetings* for a sample monthly progress form.

The committee member in charge of sending out and collecting the monthly progress forms can be the same committee member who tracks attendance at the monthly group meetings. An easy way to do this is to send each mentorship program participant a blank progress form the first of each month, requesting that they complete and return it within one week after receiving it.

Monthly Reminders

Participants with time management issues may neglect to send in their monthly progress form. Following up as often as it takes to receive their completed form is a good investment of the mentorship committee member's time.

Usually, it only takes one or two months of frequent follow up on forgotten forms to convince these participants that it is simpler to make time to do the task than to procrastinate and be reminded over and over to send in their completed progress form.

We Have A Problem...

In addition to tracking ongoing progress, monthly progress forms also serve to identify ineffective mentor-mentee pairs.

Some mentors and mentees use the forms to vent their frustrations about the relationship, such as not listening, taking too much of the other's time, constantly re-scheduling meetings, being late, or just not coming to the meetings at all.

Receiving a monthly progress form from both the mentor and the mentee allows the mentorship committee member to pinpoint issues and take action to help them resolve their differences.

As previously mentioned, having specific complaints identified on the monthly progress forms makes it imperative for the mentorship committee to act to resolve the issues if at all possible.

Given the close nature of the relationships within the mentorship program, a dysfunctional mentor-mentee pair affects far more than just those two people. The negativity surrounding a mentor-mentee pair is also apparent to the rest of the mentorship program participants.

With negative reports, the mentorship committee understandably becomes concerned about how to deal with the situation. Whether they act to resolve the issue, and how, is noted by every participant.

In addition, the level of trust between the participants in the mentorship program is directly proportional to how proactive and open the mentorship committee is in dealing with a dysfunctional mentor-mentee relationship.

"Forgotten" Progress Forms

A problem may surface when one or both of participants in a mentor-mentee pair repeatedly "forget" to complete or send in their monthly progress form. The mentorship committee member in charge of the monthly progress forms must take notice when this happens.

Forgotten forms may indicate a bigger and yet far more subtle issue than if someone uses their progress form as a way to complain about the problems in their mentoring relationship.

In these cases, the mentoring relationship may be ineffective, and one or both of the participants may be unwilling to admit this to each other and the mentorship committee. Ineffective mentoring relationships are very likely to experience early closure. Before it happens, the mentorship committee member or mentorship program leader should intervene and attempt to resolve the situation.

For all these reasons, it is important to send out the monthly progress, follow up to be sure they are received, and to follow up on any that report a problem with the mentor-mentee relationship.

Monthly Program Meetings Summary

In this chapter, we covered coordinating monthly mentorship meetings, selecting meeting topics, and monitoring the progress of the mentor-mentee pairs.

Facilitating the monthly meetings and monitoring the participants' attendance and progress forms requires a number of details to be accomplished every month of the mentorship program.

Even though it may seem daunting at the beginning, this list of tasks each month soon becomes routine for the mentorship committee.

Make no mistake, though – even if some details seem obvious or unimportant, they all combine to make the mentorship program flow smoothly for the participants from the training session through the end of the program.

Chapter 8
PROGRAM COMPLETION

The purpose of this chapter is to detail the process of ending your mentorship program for the year.

Much has changed since your 12-month journey began.

For participants, the end of the mentorship program is a time to celebrate their achievements and plan the next phase of their career development.

For the mentorship committee, it's their time to evaluate progress made over the past year and plan for the future.

Though it might seem a long way off, just two months after the end of your first mentorship program is when you need to start planning your mentorship program for the next year.

That's why it's important to take time and reflect on lessons learned at each step at the end of the program. You will then have that information to use in the planning process for your mentorship program the following year.

Time for Closure

Once the monthly group meetings begin, everyone in the program settles into the rhythm of the schedule. They attend the monthly group meetings and work on the development plan established with their mentor or mentee, and the months pass quickly.

This is especially true during the summer months. The season changes and suddenly, it's September. At that point, your participants will almost certainly be shocked to realize there are only two months left in the mentorship program.

Even though they understand the four phases of the mentoring relationship and realize Closing is the final phase, in September most of the participants are surprised that the end of their mentorship program is coming quickly.

For that very reason, begin announcing the end of the mentorship program at each of the last three monthly group meetings.

This gives all the participants time to start and finish their closure process with their mentor or mentee.

They have time to assess their progress and decide what goals are left to complete. The mentor-mentee pairs have time to get together one or two more times before the final program meeting.

Those meetings are a good time to acknowledge and appreciate the progress made during the mentorship program.

Different Ways to Close

Each mentor-mentee pair is unique. How they define their relationship both during and after the mentorship program is completely up to them.

Some mentorship pairs can't or won't wait for the end of the program and end early.

Other mentor-mentee pairs are productive throughout the program and gracefully end their professional relationship at the final program meeting.

Many of your mentor-mentee pairs may continue their professional relationship long after the final mentorship program meeting.

It's also fairly common for a mentor to provide a reference for a past mentee if asked.

One way to remain connected within the mentorship group is through LinkedIn. You may want to set up a LinkedIn group for the mentorship program, with only your mentorship participants invited to join the group.

That's one of the ways everyone can keep up with the other participants in their mentorship program after it has ended.

Final Program Planning

It's a Party!

Getting ready for the final mentorship meeting needs to start earlier than you would begin organizing the other monthly meetings.

You may find that from your very first mentorship program meeting, everyone involved in the mentorship program began thinking of the final meeting as a party. There's a good reason for this.

Both the participants and the committee members invest a large amount of energy and time into the program during the year. It's fitting that your last program meeting is designed to celebrate the hard work and achievements of everyone involved.

All of us appreciate the chance to reflect on our accomplishments. It's even more rewarding to celebrate your accomplishments with others who understand the effort involved. This day only comes once a year, so plan it out, have fun, and embrace the celebration!

Mind the Meeting Location

Hopefully, the last meeting of the mentorship program is scheduled at the same location as all your other mentorship program meetings.

Something to keep in mind, however, is that the last meeting is a celebration. For many people, celebrations include alcoholic beverages.

If your usual meeting location does not allow alcoholic beverages on site, the mentorship committee needs to choose whether to hold the party at the usual venue with no alcohol, or find another location without the same restrictions.

During the first year of your mentorship program, your mentorship program meetings may be in public facilities, such as a library or municipal building. Both venues typically have a strict no-alcohol policy. If so, you may hear a little grumbling from the participants about the lack of alcohol if you choose to have your last program meeting in your usual location.

However, the participants may also request that you move the celebration somewhere with a less stringent policy about alcoholic beverages.

One of the participants might be able to host the party at their office, complete with alcoholic beverages. And even if you change the location of the final meeting to accommodate the request for alcohol, you may find that not much is actually consumed at the event.

If you decide to offer champagne or a combination of alcoholic beverages at the final program meeting it certainly adds complexity.

Someone on the mentorship committee needs to verify if the venue allows alcoholic beverages. Also, check the local laws around liquor permits and liability. Last, take the time to find out if there are any mentors or mentees who might be offended or for whom alcohol is unhealthy.

Consider all this information in the decision whether to change the location and serve alcohol at the party.

Refreshments, Plus

Another difference between the final program meeting and the monthly group meetings are the refreshments provided.

Because it is a combined group meeting, at least two mentorship program participants (a mentor and a mentee) have committed to providing refreshments. As usual, the mentorship committee member in charge of planning the monthly program meetings should send both participants a reminder one week prior to the meeting.

Then, for this meeting, we suggest you ask the participants who signed up to provide snacks and non-alcoholic beverages for the entire group. Then the chapter can provide the rest of the refreshments for the party: cake, champagne, and any other add-ons to help with the celebration.

Gifts

You may have chosen to set aside money in the mentorship program budget to purchase gifts for the participants.

If so, they are distributed by the mentorship program leader at the final program meeting.

However, if you have concerns about the cost of creating your mentorship program, this is a good place to save chapter funds without offending anyone.

The mentorship committee invests a lot of time planning and running the mentorship program; certainly, by the final program meeting, the participants are very aware of the efforts made by each member of the mentorship committee.

For this reason, you could argue that both the chapter and the mentorship committee have already invested a great deal of time and energy in the professional development of the mentors and mentees, and an additional gift for each participant is unnecessary.

One option, and a way to limit the size of the mentorship program budget, is to give gifts only to the mentors. They devote time and energy to their mentee and the mentorship program, sometimes far beyond the program requirements. Receiving a gift at the final program meeting is a nice way for the chapter to say thank you to each mentor for their investment in the future of the chapter and its members. Mentors who volunteer each year particularly appreciate this gesture.

We have experimented with giving no gifts, giving gifts only to the mentors, and giving gifts to all participants. What we've found is it's not necessarily the gift, but the recognition of a job well done that matters most to everyone participating in the mentorship program.

Different Roles, Different Rewards

If you do decide to give gifts to both mentees and mentors, we suggest giving the two groups different gifts. We offer this advice after trying several different ways of expressing the chapter's appreciation for the mentors' time and energy.

During the first years of our mentorship program, all the participants received the same gift at the final program meeting, such as a business development book. The mentorship committee wanted to illustrate the idea that everyone can be a lifelong learner. The book choice of the end-of-program gift was paid for by the chapter.

After several years of giving everyone the same gift, the mentorship committee decided they wanted the mentors to feel appreciated for all their time and hard work throughout the program, and chose different gifts for the mentors and the mentees.

The gift mentees now receive at the end of our program is still a book on a professional topic, to encourage them to continue their career development after the mentorship program is over. If you decide to do this, someone on the mentorship committee needs to order the books at least two weeks before the final program meeting to be sure they arrive in time.

Gifts for the mentors are different. The mentors' gifts are intended to celebrate their contribution to their mentee, to the mentorship program, and to the chapter. They freely give of their time and HR knowledge for an entire year, with no expectations of any return. To show your appreciation we suggest you make sure the mentor gifts are special.

We have tried several types of mentor gifts. Believe it or not, the gifts most appreciated by our mentors are Amazon® gift cards. They like being able to spend them on anything they choose. And no matter where they live or work, Amazon delivers. The gift cards are incredibly easy to redeem, and they never expire.

Make sure the mentors' gift cards are ordered in plenty of time to arrive before the final program meeting, and are of a high enough value that the mentors can buy something they really want and might not otherwise purchase for themselves.

Final Meeting Agenda

The mentorship program leader leads the final program meeting.

It's your choice whether to have a formal recognition program at the last meeting, or simply a final meeting with no structure at all, just a party. When we tried the recognition format, it was a little difficult to keep everyone's attention on the formalities. Mostly they wanted to say goodbye to everyone and mingle.

Conversely, in the years when we had no structure to the meeting, everyone seemed to be waiting for the mentorship program leader to make some sort of speech acknowledging the end of the program.

You may want to settle on some sort of middle ground: give the participants some structure at the final program meeting without it getting in the way of the celebration. Set the expectation in advance that there will be a small amount of pomp and circumstance, with a short speech by the mentorship program leader. Then after the speech, you can begin the party.

Because the mentorship program leader leads every group meeting, the participants expect them to speak at the final program meeting. They are also acknowledged by the chapter as the leader of the mentorship program. Everyone looks to them as an authority figure, and their words and actions are very visible to all the program participants. A speech by the mentorship program leader at the final meeting, followed by a party, makes it clear to everyone that the mentorship program really is over for that year.

We're all human, and we all appreciate the recognition of a job well done. For that reason, the mentorship program leader may decide to include a short recap of everything that has happened since the beginning of that year's program in their closing speech.

With between 10–30 participants in your mentorship program, you'll find it remarkable how many of them changed jobs, received promotions, or moved to the next level in their career. Acknowledging their progress gives everyone a sense of accomplishment and the feeling that their time was well spent.

Another important component of the closing speech is to acknowledge that the work of each participant in the mentorship program need not end with the final program meeting.

The goal of nearly every participant in the mentorship program is their own professional development. The mentorship program leader's speech should include a reminder that the end of the formal program doesn't mean they should stop pursuing their professional goals. With that thought, the mentorship participants will probably be ready for the party to begin.

Even with all the work, preparation, and meetings that go into the mentorship program, the party may not last the entire two hours. After the closing speech and about thirty minutes of mingling, everyone will probably start saying their goodbyes.

Certificates of Recognition

You may decide to provide a certificate of recognition to the participants acknowledging their successful completion of the mentorship program requirements. If so, the mentorship program leader can distribute the participants' certificates and gifts immediately after their speech.

SHRM makes a certificate of recognition that is available to affiliated chapters. You can customize it with each participant's name and the dates of the mentorship program.

For the mentors, it serves another purpose as part of the documentation required to claim HRCI recertification credit for their participation in the mentorship program.

Note: See Appendix G: Program Completion *for a sample of the Certificate of Recognition. It can also be downloaded from the Resources Download area.*

Program Evaluations

The last part of the program leader's final speech is to ask the mentorship program participants to complete an evaluation form. You will probably find there are enough differences in the program each year that it helps to an evaluation form to gauge the value of the program components rather than to compare differences year-over-year.

If you decide to use one, make sure the form is easy and fast to complete. This encourages everyone to complete an evaluation form and turn it in before they leave the meeting.

Note: See Appendix G: Program Completion *for a sample of the evaluation form. It can also be downloaded from the Resources Download area.*

Professional Recognition

Something you will want to consider even in the first year of your mentorship program is to take time during a chapter meeting to formally recognize the participants who completed the mentorship program.

There are many reasons for this.

- It emphasizes the time and effort needed to complete the mentorship program.

- It gives the participants a chance to shine in front of their professional network.

- Last, but not least, it reminds chapter members interested in participating that the application period is about to open for the following year's program.

There are many ways to recognize your mentorship program participants. Some hinge on the size of your chapter and the number of participants in the program that year.

If you are a small chapter, you may ask the president to call each participant personally and offer their congratulations.

Another idea might be to publish the names of the participants in the chapter newsletter.

If you have a chapter website, use space on the home page for your recognition announcement.

Let your imagination be your guide, and try every method you can think of the first year. Some will create more of a stir than others. Remember what works best for the following year, and then add new ways to the list!

With a calendar-year mentorship program, the chapter recognition can be scheduled for your November chapter meeting. Set the date for the end of the mentorship program a few days prior to that chapter meeting, so the chapter recognition comes within a week or so after the final mentorship program meeting. The additional acknowledgement following so soon after the end of the mentorship program reinforces the sense of accomplishment participants feel about finishing the program.

Another way to recognize participants who complete the mentorship program is to post a message on the chapter's LinkedIn group page.

Ask your mentorship program leader to post the message within a few days of the program completion, and before the monthly chapter meeting. That way, even if they don't attend the monthly chapter meeting, everyone who is a member of the LinkedIn group can post a comment congratulating the mentorship program participants.

It's a Process

Setting up the chapter recognition process should begin immediately after the mentorship program ends. The mentorship program leader needs to send a message to the current chapter president with two requests.

The first request is that "Reserved" signs be placed on two or three tables at the chapter meeting near the podium at the front of the room.

The second request of the chapter president is for the mentorship program leader to make a two to three minute announcement at the chapter meeting before the program begins.

The mentorship program leader also sends an email to all the participants in the program that year reminding them they will be recognized at the chapter meeting that month. They are reminded to sit at the tables reserved for the mentorship program participants at the front of the meeting room.

On the day of the November chapter meeting, the mentorship committee should arrive early to direct the mentorship program participants to the reserved table(s). Since some or all of the committee members may have also been mentors, they should sit with the other participants at the reserved table(s).

Our experience has been that a few of the participants, or some of the mentorship committee, feel uncomfortable sitting in the front of the room.

It is the job of the mentorship program leader to remind them the chapter wishes to recognize them for their effort as part of the mentorship program that year, and to encourage them to sit with the other participants at the front of the room.

Then, when the mentorship program leader asks the mentorship program participants to stand, it is very noticeable. There is always a round of applause, and even your shyest participants will beam with pride to see their fellow HR professionals honoring them.

Another benefit of the chapter recognition is it allows senior HR professionals to become familiar with the names and faces of emerging HR professionals in your chapter. These HR leaders understand the commitment to professional development needed for a mentee to complete the mentorship program.

You might also encourage all the mentorship program participants to include their mentorship participation on their LinkedIn profile. A hiring manager who is a member of your chapter may remember if a former mentee applies for a job. In addition, the hiring manager will see on LinkedIn that the applicant participated in the mentorship program.

Time to Debrief

After the program is over for the year, the mentorship committee should hold one final meeting to review the evaluation forms and develop a sense of what worked and what elements of the program need improvement for the following year.

Most important, through the evaluation forms your participants will provide ideas for new meeting topics or ways to make an existing component work better.

The speed mentoring process came from a participant's suggestion to find a way to make the matching process more effective. This one comment set the stage for one of the foundations of our mentoring program. You will find that every year at least one great idea will come from the participants' evaluation forms.

The last mentorship committee meeting should be scheduled as soon as possible after the mentorship program ends.

Ideally it will be within two weeks after the final mentorship program meeting. This helps everyone remember events such as the speed mentoring session or the various presentations. Even so, things that happened early in the program may be difficult for the mentorship committee members to recall.

The primary goal for the meeting is to review the program evaluation forms completed by the participants. Provide a list of all the program activities at the top of the evaluation form to help participants give feedback on all parts of the mentorship program.

Leave space on the second page for participants to list the activities they found most useful, as well as activities they feel need improvement.

You should also leave plenty of space for comments.

The mentorship program participants are very honest about their experiences in the mentorship program, and will nearly always include comments and their opinions. They frequently provide great ideas for new meeting topics and ideas for ways to make the program better.

Using the evaluation forms as the basis for discussion, the mentorship committee should pay special attention to the open-ended comments.

This discussion naturally leads to making a list of things to add or do differently in the next program. If most of the mentorship committee plans to volunteer the following year, the debriefing meeting can become the first planning meeting for the next mentorship program.

If the mentorship program leader is not leading the program the following year, do your best to have a new mentorship program leader selected before the debriefing meeting. It is an ideal time for the new mentorship leader to step in and lead the discussion. That way the mentorship committee has the advantage of hearing the thoughts of both the current and the future mentorship program leaders. Starting the planning process for the next program right away also helps the mentorship committee stay focused, with plenty of time to prepare for next year's program.

Something to consider is whether to invite any new mentorship committee members to the debriefing meeting.

New committee members will find it helpful to hear feedback from the recent participants before starting to plan for the next year. If the new committee members can attend the meeting, start the planning process for the following year right away.

The only real reason not to start the planning process at the debriefing meeting is if the new committee members cannot attend. In that case, it would be a courtesy to wait and schedule another meeting to start planning for the next year with their input.

Last, but certainly not least, meeting right after the program ends gives the mentorship committee a chance for closure as a group.

This is important, since they have been working together as a team for almost a year. During that time, they have planned, facilitated, and completed a complex program for between 6 – 30 chapter members. They've been through deadlines, drama, and spent a lot of time making sure the mentorship program ran smoothly.

At the end of the debriefing meeting, it's a good idea for the mentorship program leader to say a few words in appreciation of everyone on the mentorship committee. They deserve the recognition, and for each committee member it feels good to know their hard work and time invested on behalf of the chapter was appreciated.

Chapter 9
KEY LEARNINGS

This chapter is included to emphasize key information mentioned elsewhere in the book.

You may have already decided there are certain parts that aren't practical for you, or some that you absolutely must include in your program.

Just in case you haven't already noted certain topics as being essential to the success of your mentorship program, they are included here for your consideration one more time.

Whether or not you use everything in this book during your first mentorship program is up to you.

After the first year, you will definitely want to try new ideas that you think will add value to your program.

If you find something to add that was amazing, please let us know! The beauty of programs like these is there is no limit to your creativity in adding value for your participants.

Yearlong Interview

Start counseling the mentees during the application process to treat the mentorship program like a year-long job interview, because it is. With the incredible potential for expanding their professional network, tell mentees to treat their participation in the mentorship program as though they were interviewing for a job. This advice is meant to apply to every aspect of the mentorship program. Mentees who take this advice seriously are noticeable in how they participate in the mentorship program. Consciously or unconsciously, most mentors have usually done enough recruiting and are skilled at identifying mentees who are serious about making the most of their career opportunities.

Speed Mentoring

Without a doubt, speed mentoring is a cornerstone of a successful mentorship program. This technique helps to make the relationship between the mentor-mentee pairs much stronger. The success of your first speed mentoring session will encourage you to try something new each year. Be innovative!

Informational Interviews

As a formal meeting topic in the program, informational interviews add value in several ways.

First, they help mentors emphasize the importance of doing informational interviews when meeting with their mentees.

Second, mentees who follow through and take advantage of this opportunity tend to be more successful. Be sure to add this topic to one of the combined meetings so every participant has the chance to give it a try.

As your mentorship program evolves over the years, you will see the mentees who embrace informational interviews become more comfortable in their own job interviews.

Acting It Out

There are so many ways adding this one technique makes a difference in your mentorship program.

It illustrates for the mentees that mentors (and other senior HR professionals) really do have a sense of humor.

It's a way for the mentors to have fun with their participation in the program.

For your introverted participants, it may be just the thing they need to become more comfortable with the other group members.

And seeing a legal situation acted out guarantees the mentees will never forget how to handle that situation in their career. You may not be able to include this the first year of your mentorship program. If not, try adding it as soon as you can so everyone can have fun with it.

Geography

Sometimes no matter how much someone wants to participate in the mentorship program, geography works against them.

This is true for individuals as well as the mentor-mentee pairs. Work to mitigate the effect of geography; make sure you consider location when pairing mentors and mentees to help them avoid driving more than 20 – 30 miles to meet.

Caution people who live a long distance from the monthly meeting venue that their energy and enthusiasm may be taxed from working all day, driving two hours to a meeting, and then driving home again.

Despite all efforts, geography can present issues with participation. Provide fair warning to participants on this topic while offering encouragement for those with a long commute.

Mentor Quads

It seems so simple, yet the value-add for the mentors with this addition can be profound.

It really does take a village to raise a mentee.

Having other HR professionals to talk with who understand the process and the challenges involved in mentoring someone has become central to the satisfaction of our mentors. Sometimes in an HR department of one, you just need to talk it out with someone who has experienced the same set of circumstances.

The Devil Really Is In the Details

Once the training session is complete, the heart of your mentorship program – the monthly mentoring meetings – begin.

This is where the program's true value lies for the participants. Hold strong through the summer vacation season and keep the program mentors, mentees, and program committee on course.

Your attention to the schedule and details of running the mentorship program will provide others with a role model for committing and completing the program. The results will speak for themselves, and everyone wins.

Communicate, Communicate, Communicate

You probably have no doubt by now about the importance of communication in your mentorship program, but it bears repeating.

Communication is the glue that keeps the program running.

This is true in all aspects of the program.

The mentorship program leader needs to communicate with the mentorship committee.

The mentorship committee members need to communicate with each other.

The committee members must communicate with the participants.

The participants need to communicate with each other each month at the meetings. And most important, the mentor-mentee pairs need to talk with each other regularly.

When all of these communication channels are open, the mentorship program is most effective. The program goal of providing professional development is realized, and people's lives are changed.

Serendipity

Making a commitment to change your professional life puts other changes in motion. No matter how committed someone is to the mentorship program, life happens and things change. Be it a new job, a new city, or a different profession, quality relationships within the mentorship program help participants be successful in moving onto their next phase.

Think Big

The work you do here isn't just about starting a mentorship program to help emerging professionals in your chapter.

It's much, much bigger.

A mentorship program creates many positive changes within your whole chapter.

Participants will have stronger relationships after the program, stay in touch with each other, and celebrate each other's' successes.

The mentees' confidence in their HR knowledge will grow exponentially, giving way to greater confidence.

Best of all, the mentorship program will be instrumental in developing a succession plan for your chapter.

Senior HR professionals will become more involved in the chapter.

Former mentees will volunteer on committees, creating a natural career path toward serving on the board of directors and the leadership team.

Starting a mentorship program helps your entire chapter.

Chapter 10
TESTIMONIALS

This section is included so you can read about the positive changes participants experience in a mentorship program. We asked some of our previous mentorship participants to describe the benefit(s) they gained from their participation in the program. Below are their unedited comments.

In Their Own Words

"My goals at the time were to learn more about recertification, learn how to get published within the field, get general guidance about some pretty complex work issues, learn what resources are out there for HR professionals, and gain a bit of confidence – my self-doubt had gotten the most of me and I had felt like maybe I didn't deserve the certification I had worked so hard for. By the time the program wrapped up, I had accomplished what I had set out to do. I'm on track for recertification, I've found a few different avenues for getting my writing out into the HR community, I received some great feedback on tackling tricky workplace situations, I built up a wonderful network of resources, and I finally have the confidence to say that I deserved to get my SPHR and that I deserve a seat at the table. I wouldn't have been able to do all of these things if it weren't for the mentorship program, and really the entire group, most of whom I've been lucky enough to still stay in touch with. I am grateful for the opportunity I got and hope to pay it back in the future by mentoring others in the field." – S.L.

"In addition to the guidance and support we gained from our mentors, our fellow mentees have served as sounding boards and idea caches to help us on our paths forward. The mentorship program content was extremely valuable in preparatory issues such as creating our LinkedIn sites and branding, items that prepare us for our future employment within human resources. It was an extremely rewarding group to belong to and it is my hope that the connections that I have made will continue forward." - R.M.

"I have been fortunate to have been part of the Mentorship Program because I have met amazing professional people. I have learned so much about how important is to give and share with others. When I think of a word to describe the program, "Generosity" is the one that comes to my mind. The program is a unique developmental opportunity and I feel very lucky to have been part of the group of mentees. I have learned a great deal about HR practices and I am certain that the knowledge and skills I have acquired will be of value throughout my career." – D.M.

"For me it's been the professional networking that's been invaluable. Collectively the breadth and depth of the HR experience and pool of skills are a gold mine, and the openness in the group to share one another's expertise has been incredible. It's been a great experience and I hope to be part of this again in the future." – D.S.

"I would like to share two things – first the support the program provides for the mentee, and second the support the program provides for the mentor.

1. Mentor/Mentee Relationship: I served, with pride, for two years of service with the Mentorship Program as a mentor. The initial connection to our mentees was a brilliant process in the form of Speed Mentorship. I loved the way this kicked off the year and for me, the mentee/mentor relationship I had with both my mentees was a perfect match which set the tone for the entire program each year. It was such an instrumental start and I believe both my mentees' success in finding more robust HR roles can be directly attributed to the strength of this introduction.

2. Mentor Support: A huge impact for me personally was the strength of the networking among our program peers. During this time, I would say that my networking circle nearly doubled, starting with the mentorship program and branching out into the HR industry locally, regionally, and even nationally. Some of my closest industry friends came directly from the mentor subgroup of our program and continue to be an active part of my HR world. In fact, several of us still meet regularly outside the program, to catch up on challenges in our workplaces as well as to share career leads. Invaluable." – R.P.

"For me the most satisfying part about being a mentor is being able to share my past experiences and provide a source of support, advice, and inspiration to other HR Professionals. I am fortunate to get to develop meaningful relationships with my mentees in which I can assist in developing specific skills and knowledge that will enhance their professional and personal growth. Being a mentor has also taught me to become more outgoing, articulate, and confident. Leadership and communication skills are invaluable and the mentorship program has helped me enhanced these skills. It has also allowed me to connect with other seasoned HR professionals and be part of a mentorship team that provides support for me and allows me to support them in turn." – K.E.

"This is my second year as a mentor in the mentorship program… and I love it! On an individual level, mentorship provides a tremendous opportunity for personal and professional growth. I've learned an incredible amount from my mentee and fellow mentors. Those relationships have truly helped me get to the next level. From a big picture perspective, participating in the mentorship program provides the chance to contribute to the HR profession. I'm able to make a difference in the life of someone new to HR, which strengthens our profession overall." – S.D.

APPENDICES

The appendices provided here are samples and supplemental information for your use in running your mentorship program. The appendices are organized by the book chapter where they first appear.

APPENDIX A: GOAL SETTING AND PLANNING

Job Description: Mentorship Program Leader

Qualifications

The candidate for mentorship program leader is outgoing, with skill in personal networking and starting new programs. You are experienced at leading others and running meetings, a strong communicator, and have a strong desire to provide career development opportunities for other HR professionals. Qualifications for the mentorship program leader:

- Active chapter member
- Minimum of 5 years of HR experience. This can be a combination of HR management, generalist, consultant, or a specialist role (i.e., benefits, compensation, recruitment, etc.)
- Knowledgeable about current HR practices
- Skilled in preparing and managing budgets
- Experienced leader; demonstrated familiarity in planning and organizing the work of others, delegating and managing deadlines.
- Willing to make a 12-month commitment to the mentorship program, program committee, and mentorship participants.

Mentorship Program Leader Role

In the role of mentorship program leader, you will plan, organize and direct other committee members throughout the entire mentorship program. You will lead the committee members, mentors, and mentees participating in the mentorship program. You have the above qualifications and are capable of carrying out the following responsibilities:

- Write mentorship committee job descriptions.

- Recruit and select mentorship committee members.

- Work with the chapter board of directors and mentorship committee to decide the program details, budget, and marketing plan.

- Schedule mentorship program meetings, decide program content and speaker schedule, and conduct committee and mentoring meetings.

- Communicate with mentorship program participants regarding acceptance and expectations.

- Schedule and conduct mentorship program training session.

- Facilitate ongoing mentorship program activities.

- Evaluate participant feedback and progress reports for early signs of closure with mentor-mentee pairs.

- Lead brainstorming sessions and all program-end activities.

- Plan, prepare, and conduct a chapter recognition event.

Job Description: Mentorship Committee Member

Qualifications

The candidate for mentorship committee member is a team player with attention to detail, enthusiastic about working with others, cooperative, a strong communicator, and has a strong desire to provide career development opportunities for other HR professionals. Qualifications for the mentorship committee member:

- Active chapter member
- Minimum of 5 years of HR experience. This can be a combination of HR management, generalist, consultant, or a specialist role (i.e., benefits, compensation, recruitment, etc.)
- Knowledgeable about current HR practices
- Willing to make a 12-month commitment to the mentorship program, program committee, and mentorship participants
- Readily available by phone and/or email throughout the entire mentorship program

Mentorship Committee Member Role

You will plan, organize, and assist other committee members to facilitate professional growth for a group of chapter members. The individual filling this role will demonstrate that he or she has the right qualifications and is capable of carrying out the following responsibilities:

- Work with other committee members to develop the mentorship program marketing plan.
- Assist the mentorship program leader and other mentorship committee members with planning and preparing for mentorship program activities.
- Participate in the participant selection process for both mentors and mentees. Conduct interviews and review results of mentor and mentee candidates.
- Assist the mentorship program leader and other mentorship committee members with planning and preparing meeting activities.
- Participate in mentoring program activities, discussions and tracking of program progress.
- May conduct committee meetings and provide follow-up assistance to the committee and/or mentorship program leader.
- Assist in planning and preparation for the chapter recognition event.

APPENDIX B: MARKETING

Sample Program Requirements

Below is a sample of the mentorship program requirements. Note that job descriptions for both the mentor and the mentee are included in this sample.

20xx Mentorship Program
20XX <Chapter Name> Mentorship Program

Our chapter is seeking exceptional human resources professionals to participate in our mentorship program.

Who We Are:

- The <Chapter Name> Mentorship Program is a developmental partnership through which the mentor shares their knowledge, skills, information and perspective to foster the professional growth of the mentee.

- The purpose of the Mentorship Program is to support the chapter's objective of furthering the ongoing enhancement of a dynamic, diverse membership and, as a result, the HR profession through learning and networking.

- We give senior-level HR professionals an opportunity to "give back" to our members and our profession through a one of a kind opportunity for collaboration, goal achievement and problem solving.

Who You Are:

Mentor

You facilitate professional growth for another individual by sharing the knowledge and insights you have learned throughout your years as a Human Resources Professional. You are able to carry out the responsibilities and meet the requirements listed below:

- Active <Chapter Name> member.

- Minimum of five years of HR experience. This can be a combination of HR management, generalist, consultant, or a specialist role (i.e., benefits, compensation, recruitment, etc.)

- Willingness to make a 10-month commitment, starting in January, to your mentee with at least one hour per month in face-to-face meetings.

- Completion of the <Chapter Name> Mentorship Program progress form after your monthly meetings.

- Available by phone and/or email throughout the month to your mentee, typically for non-urgent or not time sensitive consultations.

- Attendance at monthly group meetings in addition to regular meetings in smaller mentor sub-groups.

- SPHR/PHR or a specialization certification preferred, though not required.

Mentee

You are an achiever seeking developmental advancement through opportunities to learn and excel. You are able to carry out the responsibilities and meet the requirements listed below:

- Active <Chapter Name> member.
- Dedicated professional wishing to gain additional knowledge and information in human resources.
- Willingness to make a 10-month commitment, starting in January, to your mentor with at least one hour per month in face-to-face meetings.
- Completion of the <Chapter Name> Mentorship Program progress form after monthly meetings.
- Attendance at monthly group meetings in addition to face-to-face meetings with your mentor.

How to apply:

If you believe you are the right individual to fill one of these roles, please submit your cover letter and current résumé to mentors@<Chapter Name>.org.

Your cover letter should include:

- Your name and any professional designations
- Contact phone number(s)
- Email address(s)
- Home/work addresses
- Name of your company or organization
- A description of your human resources background
- Three goals you have for the mentorship program
- Important aspects you are looking for in a mentor/mentee partner
- Your three greatest strengths and three areas that need most improvement

Mentors: Please include in the subject line: "20XX <Chapter Name> Mentorship Program – Mentor Application". Deadline for submitting your cover letter and résumé is <Date>, **20XX**.

Mentees: Please include in the subject line: "20XX <Chapter Name> Mentorship Program – Mentee Application". Deadline for submitting your cover letter and résumé is <Date>, **20XX**.

Please Note:
For the 20XX <Chapter Name> Mentorship Program
we will be accepting a maximum of 15 mentors and 15 mentees.
Apply now!

APPENDIX C: PARTICIPANT SELECTION

Sample Mentor Candidate Interview Email

Below is a sample email for scheduling an interview with a mentor candidate.

Thank you for submitting your application to be a mentor in this year's mentorship program. The next step in the process is to meet with one of the mentorship committee members to complete an interview that will determine who will be selected as a mentor for this year.

<Mentorship Committee Member> will be contacting you to set up a time for you to meet at your earliest convenience. Thank you for your interest in this program. If you have any questions, please don't hesitate to call me or just reply to this message.

Thank you,

<Mentorship Program Leader>
<Phone number>

Mentor Interview Questions

1. What motivated you to apply to our program?

2. What do you hope to gain from this experience?

3. How would you describe the role of a mentee? What does the mentee-mentor relationship look like to you?

4. Tell me about a time when you have been mentored/coached by someone. What was the outcome?

5. What do you do when you're upset with someone?

6. Our mentorship program is a big commitment, with group monthly meetings, individual coaching sessions and homework. How do you feel about that?

Selection Factors for Mentors

At the end of the mentor interview process, discuss each applicant with the mentorship committee. As each member reviews their notes, enter the score into the Mentor Selection Factors worksheet. The goal is as high a number as possible for selection as a mentee in the program.

1. Rate each candidate on a 1 – 5 scale for each selection factor; 1 = low; 5 = high.

2. Total each selection factor and calculate the average for that factor.

3. Enter the average score for each selection factor in the spreadsheet.

4. Total the score of all factors for each applicant.

5. Repeat the above steps for each applicants

Once the score for all the applicants have been totaled, the spreadsheet is sorted by the score totals. This makes it immediately apparent if there are any trends in the applicants' score totals.

Below is an example of the spreadsheet to use for scoring the applicants. This spreadsheet is available in the Resources Download area.

Selection Factors

Mentor Name	Program Commitment	HR Commitment	Relationship Understanding	Personal Responsibility	Self-Improvement	Difficult Conversation	Years HR Experience	TOTAL	Interviewer Comments
Elisa Eckart									
Daron Dasilva									
Joleen Jonason									

Selection Factor	Description
Program Commitment	Has the candidate said they can attend the meetings? Does the candidate understand the overall commitment? Has the candidate ever shown similar commitment to a volunteer or educational program?
HR Profession Commitment	Do the candidate's goals align with a future career in HR? What has the candidate done (so far) to engage in the HR profession (classes, certificate, internship, job, chapter volunteer)?
Understands Mentor-Mentee relationship	Does the candidate understand that mentors are coaches? Has the candidate been in some type of mentoring relationship?
Personal Responsibility	Does the candidate take ownership for his/her own actions?
Self-Improvement	Has the candidate exhibited an interest in learning (continuing with school, classes, projects)? Does the candidate seem introspective and committed to self-improvement?
Difficult Conversations	Has the candidate had to deal with emotionally charged or difficult conversations? Does the candidate engage or ignore problems with others?
Comfort Level	
HR Experience	How many years of hands-on HR experience does the candidate have?

Sample Mentor Pre-Meeting Message

Below is a sample of an email you can send to mentors informing them of their acceptance into your mentorship program and letting them know of the Mentor Pre-Meeting.

Congratulations on your selection as a mentor for this year's mentorship program. The first meeting for mentors will be on **<Date> <Time>**in <room number> at the <location name and web address.>

The <location name> address is:

<Insert location address>

Action item: Please reply to this message and include in the subject line either "Yes, I will be there" or "No, I won't be there." Please make every effort to attend as we will be coming together as a group for the first time. Please also take a moment to check the address for this location prior to the day of the meeting so you are prepared for the transit time required to be on time.

I hope to see you there – we are really looking forward to this year's mentorship program!

Thank you,

<Mentorship Program Leader>

Sample Agenda: Mentors Get Acquainted

Below is a sample agenda for the Mentors Get Acquainted Meeting. This sample identifies the handouts you would need for the meeting and the agenda to follow during the meeting.

<LOCATION NAME>
<LOCATION ADDRESS>
Handouts

- Agenda
- Mentorship Program Meeting Dates
- Mentorship Program Requirements
- Mentor/Mentee Locations
- Mentee Interview Questions
- Mentee Selection Factors

Agenda

6 – 6:15 PM Mingle and refreshments

6:15 – 6:20 PM Introduction to the mentorship program

- Purpose of the mentorship program:
  - "Further the ongoing enhancement of a dynamic, diverse membership and, as a result, the HR profession through learning and networking"
  - Build a stronger HR community
  - Teach other HR professionals how to be "a business partner who specializes" – strategic rather than transactional

6:20 – 7:00 PM Mentor introductions

- Name
- Position
- Interest in the program
- Personal goal for the program
- Fun fact about your first HR job

7:00 – 7:30 PM Announcements, mentor sub-groups and mentee interviews

- Introduce mentorship program leader
- Meeting attendance is mandatory
- Communicate at the FIRST hint of disengagement ("it takes a village")
- Form mentor sub-groups (geographically based)
- Mentee interviews

7:30 – 7:45 PM Next meeting: Speed mentoring on <Date>@ <Time>

- Bring résumés if desired
- Treat as an informational interview (but much shorter!)

7:45 – 8 PM   Questions / Networking

Sample Mentor Candidate Interview Email

Below is a sample email for scheduling an interview with a mentee candidate.

Thank you for submitting your application to be a mentor in this year's mentorship program. The next step in the process is to meet with one of the mentorship committee members to complete an interview that will determine who will be selected as a mentee for this year.

<Mentorship Committee Member> will be contacting you to set up a time for you to meet at your earliest convenience. Thank you for your interest in this program. If you have any questions, please don't hesitate to call me or just reply to this message.

Thank you,

<Mentorship Program Leader>

<Phone number>

Selection Factors for Mentees

At the end of the mentee advisory meetings, discuss each applicant with the mentorship committee. As each member reviews their notes, enter the score into the Mentee Selection Factors worksheet. The goal is as high a number as possible for selection as a mentee in the program.

1. Rate each candidate on a 1 – 5 scale for each selection factor; 1 = low; 5 = high.

2. Total each selection factor and calculate the average for that factor.

3. Enter the average score for each selection factor in the spreadsheet.

4. Total the score of all factors for each applicant.

5. Repeat the above steps for each applicants.

Once the score for all the mentee applicants have been totaled, the spreadsheet is sorted by the score totals. This makes it immediately apparent if there are any trends in the applicants' score totals.

Below is an example of the spreadsheet to use for scoring the applicants. This spreadsheet is available in the Resources Download area.

Selection Factors

Mentee Name	Program Commitment	HR Commitment	Relationship Understanding	Personal Responsibility	Self-Improvement	Difficult Conversation	Years HR Experience	TOTAL	Comments
Marilu Mastropietro									
Jani Jonason									
Amy Ashbrook									

Selection Factor	Description
Program Commitment	Has the candidate said they can attend the meetings? Does the candidate understand the overall commitment? Has the candidate ever shown similar commitment to a volunteer or educational program?
HR Profession Commitment	Do the candidate's goals align with a future career in HR? What has the candidate done (so far) to engage in the HR profession (classes, certificate, internship, job, chapter volunteer)?
Understands Mentor-Mentee relationship	Does the candidate understand that mentors are coaches? Has the candidate been in some type of mentoring relationship?
Personal Responsibility	Does the candidate take ownership for his/her own actions?
Self-Improvement	Has the candidate exhibited an interest in learning (continuing with school, classes, projects)? Does the candidate seem introspective and committed to self-improvement?
Difficult Conversations	Has the candidate had to deal with emotionally charged or difficult conversations? Does the candidate engage or ignore problems with others?
HR Experience	How many years of hands-on HR experience does the candidate have?

Sample Mentee Pre-Meeting Message

Below is a sample of an email you would send to mentees informing them of their acceptance into your mentorship program and letting them know of the Mentee Pre-Meeting.

Congratulations on your selection as a mentee for this year's mentorship program. The first meeting for mentees will be on **<Date> <Time>** in <room number> at <location name>. The <location name> address is:

<Insert location address>

*Action item: **Please reply to this message and include in the subject line either "Yes, I will be there" or "No, I won't be there."*** Please make every effort to attend as we will be coming together as a group for the first time. Please also take a moment to check the address for this location prior to the day of the meeting so you are prepared for the transit time required to be on time.

I hope to see you there – we are looking forward to this year's mentorship program!

Thank you,

<Mentorship Program Leader>

Sample Agenda: Mentees Get Acquainted Meeting

Below is a sample agenda for the Mentees Get Acquainted Meeting. This sample identifies the handouts you would need for the meeting and the agenda to follow during the meeting.

<LOCATION NAME>
<LOCATION ADDRESS>

Handouts

- Agenda
- Mentorship Program Meeting Dates
- Mentorship Program Requirements

Agenda

6 – 6:15 PM Mingle and refreshments

6:15 – 6:20 PM Introduction to the mentorship program

- Purpose of the mentorship program:
  - "Further the ongoing enhancement of a dynamic, diverse membership and, as a result, the HR profession through learning and networking"
  - Build a stronger HR community
  - Teach other HR professionals how to be "a business partner who specializes" – strategic rather than transactional

6:20 – 7:00 PM Mentee introductions

- Name
- Position
- Interest in the program
- Personal goal for the program
- Fun fact about your first job

7:00 – 7:30 PM Announcements

- Introduce mentorship program leader
- Meeting attendance is mandatory
- Communicate at the FIRST hint of disengagement ("it takes a village")

7:30 – 7:45 PM Next meeting: Speed mentoring on <Date>@ <Time>

- Bring résumés if desired
- Treat as an informational interview (but much shorter!)

7:45 – 8 PM Questions / Networking

APPENDIX D: SPEED MENTORING SESSION

Speed Mentoring Booklet Template

Below is an example of a speed mentoring booklet looks for use when completed for both mentors and mentees during the speed mentoring process.

Mentee: Name
Title
Company
Work: City, Home: City

Bio: Award.

Important Aspects in a Mentorship Partner:

1. X

3 Goals for Mentorship Program:

1. X
2. X
3. X

3 Greatest Strengths:

1. X
2. X
3. X

3 Areas of Improvement:

1. X
2. X
3. X

Insert participant's photo here

NOTES

Sample Mentor Ballot

Below is a sample of the ballot you will give to your mentors. The mentors will use this ballot to select their top three mentee choices.

2013 Mentorship Program
Speed Mentoring Ballot
(Give to Mentors)

Name: _____

Select your top 3 choices using 1st, 2nd and 3rd next to their names.	
Jane Doe	
Jack Smith	
Mary Jane	
Jean Johnson	
Sally Who	
Patty Lynn	
Bobby Jo	
Ralph Johnson	
Jean Jones	
James Smith	
Jenny Sue	

Sample Mentee Ballot

Below is a sample of the ballot you will give to your mentees. The mentors will use this ballot to select their top three mentor choices.

2013 Mentorship Program
Speed Mentoring Ballot
(Give to Mentees)

Name: _____

Select your top 3 choices using 1st, 2nd and 3rd next to their names.	
John Doe	
Barbara Smith	
Mark Johnson	
Billy Bob	
Marcia Smith	
Susie Who	
Mary Jo	
Ronnie Jean	
Jim Jones	
Jane Smith	
Sue Smith	

Mentors Refreshment Sign-up Sheet

Below is a sample of the refreshment sign-up sheet you will ask mentors to fill out during the mentor pre-meeting.

MENTOR SNACK SIGN-UP SHEET

Meeting Date	Mentor Name
Tuesday, March 6, 20xx Speed Mentoring (Combined)	
Tuesday, March 20, 20xx Combined Meeting	
Tuesday, April 17, 20xx Mentors Meeting	
Tuesday, May 15, 20xx Combined Meeting	
Tuesday, June 12, 20xx Mentors Meeting	
Tuesday, July 10, 20xx Combined Meeting	
Tuesday, August 14, 20xx Mentors Meeting	
Tuesday, September 11, 20xx Combined Meeting	
Tuesday, October 16, 20xx Mentors Meeting	
Tuesday, November 6, 20xx Combined Meeting	

Mentees Refreshments Sign-up Sheet

Below is a sample of the refreshment sign-up sheet you will ask mentees to fill out during the mentee pre-meeting.

MENTEE SNACK SIGN-UP SHEET

Meeting Date	Mentee Name
Tuesday, March 6, 20xx Speed Mentoring (Combined)	
Tuesday, March 20, 20xx Combined Meeting	
Monday, April 16, 20xx Mentees Meeting	
Tuesday, May 15, 20xx Combined Meeting	
Monday, June 11, 20xx Mentees Meeting	
Tuesday, July 10, 20xx Combined Meeting	
Monday, August 13, 20xx Mentees Meeting	
Tuesday, September 11, 20xx Combined Meeting	
Monday, October 15, 20xx Mentees Meeting	
Tuesday, November 6, 20xx Combined Meeting	

APPENDIX E: TRAINING SESSION

Training Session Handouts

The following handouts are used during the Training Session. These handouts are also available in the Resources Download area.

Handout		Purpose of Handout
Printout of PowerPoint slides, 2 slides per page		Give participants a way to follow presentation and take notes
Preparing Phase		
1	Strategies and Considerations for Initial Conversations	Brief suggestions for participants to use when they meet the first few times
2	Mentoring Pre-Work	Best practices for mentors on how to engage their mentee in the first few conversations
3	Roles, Responsibilities…of Effective Mentors and Mentees	Information about the responsibilities of each role (mentor and mentee) for the participants to use in working out their agreement
4	Reasonable Expectations for Mentors and Mentees	Information to provide clarity on what are reasonable expectations for each partner in the mentoring relationship

Handout		Purpose of Handout
Negotiating Phase		
1	Personal Inventory Tool	A list to enter personal information that may help the mentor-mentee pairs establish common ground at the beginning of their relationship
2	Career and Life Goals	Worksheet for mentees to help establish the priorities for their mentoring relationship
3	Setting Goals	Discusses goal-setting for the mentorship program using the SMART approach
4	Development Activities for Mentees	Ideas to help mentors and mentees generate a list of the development activities they plan to use
5	Identifying Learning Opportunities	A list of different activities, to be used as a starting point for ideas to help the mentee achieve their goals
6	Generating a List of Learning Opportunities	Used to add some clarity about the purpose of different learning opportunities to be used in the mentoring relationship
7	Developing the Work Plan	A way to formalize the goals for the mentoring relationship and how they will be achieved
8	Setting Relationship Parameters	A template for describing the parameters of the mentorship agreement
9	Mentoring Partnership Agreement	A sample mentoring partnership agreement for participants to review before they create their own
10	Partnership Agreement Template	Template for creating their mentorship agreement
11	Streamlined Mentoring Partnership Agreement Template	Shortened version of the mentoring partnership agreement template
12	Readiness Checklist	Things to be checked prior to formalizing the mentoring partnership
13	Negotiating Questions and Outcomes	A list of question for use in determining if all topics have been covered in completing the partnership agreement

Handout		Purpose of Handout
Enabling Phase		
1	Mentoring Builds Great Leaders, But Only If There Is Fierce Honesty	A discussion of the importance of honesty in the mentoring relationship
2	Assessing the Partnership	A series of questions for use by both mentee and mentor to determine the health of their relationship
3	Listening and Feedback Skills	Discussion of the skills needed to ensure effective communication
4	Strategies for Overcoming Obstacles	Information for mentors on ways the relationship may be derailed
Closing Phase		
1	Signals That It Might Be Time For Closure	Warning signals about the relationship ending prematurely
2	Closure Preparation: Steps and Questions	Tool to use when approaching the end of the mentorship program
3	Closing: A Readiness Checklist	A list to be sure the relationship is ending as planned
4	Turning Closure Into Learning	A series of questions to help the mentors as they complete the relationship
Mentee-Mentor Matches List		Official list of which mentor is matched with which mentee
Meeting Topic List		List of the program meeting topics for that year's program for mentors and mentees to use as they plan their individual meetings

Training Session Conversations

Designing the Mentor-Mentee Relationship

The initial meeting between the mentor and mentee is critical to the success of the relationship, because it sets the tone of the relationship.

It is extremely important (especially if the mentor and mentee don't know each other) to take the time to create a climate of trust and safety.

The agreements made between the mentor and mentee at the first meeting provide the "container" in which the relationship will take place. The mentor and mentee design the container so that it is customized to specifically meet the needs of both. The container is dynamic, capable of changing over time so that it will continue to meet their needs and not become obsolete. The initial meeting also helps the mentor learn how to work with the mentee in a manner that empowers the mentee.

While each mentor has or will develop their own unique style, here are some guidelines to get you started:

- It may take several meetings to cover the material; how long depends on how they structure their meetings.

- It is important to have the first meeting in a neutral location away from both their offices where they have privacy and freedom from distractions.

- Ideally, it is preferable to allow an hour and a half to two hours for the initial meeting, because there is so much to cover and they will need time to build rapport.

- It is highly recommended that they take good notes during the session.

Guidelines for Mentors to Engage Their Mentee

The list below contains guidelines for how to get started with your mentee and are designed based on research of "best practices" for mentoring programs. You will not be able to cover all of these topics in one meeting, so use these questions and discussion topics to fit your own style and approach.

1. Review with your mentee what you would like to cover in the initial meeting. Ask the mentee how that sounds to them and if there is anything else they would like to cover.

2. Discuss what mentoring is and isn't.

3. Talk about why you are a mentor and what you get out of it.

4. Discuss what is confidential and what is not.

5. Ask your mentee what they would like to get out of the mentoring relationship.

6. Ask your mentee some questions to get to know more about them and what they want.

7. Ask your mentee what they would like to know about your background.

8. Review the responsibilities of mentor and mentee.

9. Ask questions about what mentee needs from you.

10. Share with your mentee what you need from them as the mentee, what's important to you in the relationship as a mentor, and how you like to work as a mentor.

11. Decide on the logistics and structures you will use to support your relationship.

12. Make some agreements based on these conversations about how you will interact with each other to best support the mentee in achieving their agenda and goals.

13. Ask your mentee if there is anything else that is important to them to cover in the session.

Close with a review of the next steps and an agreement on the location, date and time of the next meeting. (You may want to ask the mentee to review the competencies and skills for their job and identify some areas in which they would like support).

Initial Conversation with the Mentee

1. DISCUSS WHAT MENTORING IS AND ISN'T

   • The role of the mentor is to support the mentee and strengthen competencies needed to enhance job performance, as well as support them in career progression. The purpose of the relationship is to support the mentee in their agenda and career goals. (Both mentor and mentee need to have a realistic understanding and agreement of where the mentee is now and where they would like to be. Then they need to decide on the developmental activities in which the mentor needs to be involved to get where they want to go.)

- Mentoring is a partnership in which power is granted to the relationship, not the mentor. (The mentor is not the expert who tells the mentee what to do. The mentor is a partner who shares their knowledge and learnings from their work experience.)

- The mentee needs to be mindful of what they need, and if their needs are not being met, they need to let the mentor know and request what they need.

- Mentoring is a mutual learning relationship and experience.

2. TALK ABOUT WHY YOU MENTOR AND WHAT YOU GET OUT OF IT.

- If you have never mentored before, talk about what you look forward to about this process and what you would like to get from it.

3. ASK MENTEE IN GENERAL, WHAT THEY WOULD LIKE TO GET OUT OF THE RELATIONSHIP.

4. ASK MENTEE SOME QUESTIONS TO GET TO KNOW MORE ABOUT THEM AND WHAT THEY WANT. SAMPLE QUESTIONS:

- Tell me about your job: How long you been here? What do you do? Who is your supervisor? What do you like about your job? What is challenging or what don't you like about it? What are your strengths? What are the areas that you feel you need to develop skills in or learn more about?

- What do you like to do outside of work?

- Tell me about where you want to be in your career or what do you want to be doing one year from now? In three years? In five years? (Make sure mentee describes the nature of activities or work they would like to be doing, not just a job title.)

5. ASK MENTEE WHAT THEY WOULD LIKE TO KNOW ABOUT YOUR BACKGROUND.

- If mentee doesn't ask any thing, offer information about your background you think may be helpful.

6. REVIEW RESPONSIBILITIES OF MENTOR AND MENTEE.

- Ask if there are any questions about the mentee's responsibilities.

- What areas of your responsibilities do they feel would be particularly helpful to them?

7. ASK QUESTIONS ABOUT WHAT MENTEE NEEDS FROM YOU. SOME SAMPLE QUESTIONS TO ASK:

- How do you want me to interact with you as your mentor?

- What kind of support do you want from me?

- How do you like to be supported to accomplish goals? (e.g.: Forcefully pushed? Gently encouraged? Challenged? Need a lot of acknowledgement for what is working or what you are doing right in relationship to what you want?)

- What are you looking for in a coach?
- How can I best support you?
- How do you want me to be when you have not completed something you agreed to complete
- If this mentoring were to have a huge impact on your career what would it look like?

8. SHARE WITH MENTEE WHAT YOU NEED FROM THEM, WHAT'S IMPORTANT TO YOU IN THE RELATIONSHIP AS A MENTOR, AND HOW YOU LIKE TO WORK AS A MENTOR. EXAMPLES OF THE KINDS OF THINGS YOU MIGHT TALK ABOUT HERE ARE:

- Commitment to the relationship and keeping agreements you make with each other.
- Telling the truth…for example, about what you see the mentee being strong in and where you see them selling themselves short or setting themselves up.
- Being honest and direct with the mentee when something is up. (Ask if you have their permission to be direct.)
- Seeing this as a partnership and expecting the mentee to be honest and direct if a need is not getting met, something is not working for them about what you are doing or how you interact with them, or if something is bothering them.
- Asking for permission to fail or to make mistakes, if you as a mentor are new at mentoring.
- You may want to let the mentee know you will challenge them to take risks and hold them to bigger goals.
- Talk about how important CONFIDENTIALITY is and ask mentee to agree on what is to be kept confidential in your relationship.

9. DECIDE ON THE LOGISTICS AND STRUCTURES YOU WILL USE TO SUPPORT YOUR RELATIONSHIP:

- Meeting times.
- Length of meetings.
- Frequency of meetings.
- Location of meetings.
- Who initiates meetings?
- How will you structure your meetings or use your time together?
- Any forms or structures you want to use.

10. MAKE SOME AGREEMENTS BASED ON ABOVE CONVERSATIONS ABOUT HOW TO INTERACT WITH EACH OTHER TO BEST SUPPORT MENTEE IN ACHIEVING THEIR AGENDA AND GOALS.

- Make sure to include confidentiality.
- May want to sign a mentoring agreement.

11. ASK THE MENTEE IF THERE IS ANYTHING ELSE THEY WISH TO COVER?

- Any concerns they have?

12. CLOSE WITH WHAT THE NEXT STEPS ARE AND AGREE ON THE NEXT MEETING

- You may want to ask the mentee to think about where they are now and where they would like to be in the next 5 years.

- You may also want to ask the mentee to review their job competencies and/or skill requirements and come up with some goals or areas where they want support from you to help develop.

- At the next meeting, you both agree on the goals and decide on the developmental activities in which the mentor needs to be involved to get where they want to go. They can complete a mentoring action plan.

APPENDIX F: MONTHLY PROGRAM MEETINGS

Meeting Topics

Here is a list of meeting topics you may want to use for your mentorship program meetings:

Mentee Group Meetings

1. Prior mentees: Q & A on their experience as a mentee
2. Being a connector (professional networking)
3. Maximizing your LinkedIn profile
4. Personal branding
5. Case studies
6. Past presidents: Q & A on being a chapter leader / chapter volunteer opportunities

Mentor Group Meetings

1. Round robin check-ins / open mike
2. Global HR
3. Diversity and inclusion

Mentor and Mentee Combined Meetings

1. Global HR
2. Diversity and inclusion
3. Case studies with role-playing by mentors
4. Informational interview practice

Mentor-Mentee Monthly Progress Form

Below is a sample monthly progress form to use in your mentorship program.

\<Chapter Name\> Mentor and Mentee Progress Form

Mentor: _____   **Mentee:** _____

Assigned Date: _____   **First Meeting Date:**_____

Form Filled Out By: _____

Goals Mentor and Mentee set for program at first meeting:

_____

_____

_____

_____

Meeting Notes:

Month 1 Meeting Date:_____

_____

Month 2 Meeting Date:_____

_____

Month 3 Meeting Date:_____

_____

(Email to Mentorship Chair for progress check)

Month 4 Meeting Date:_____

_____

Month 5 Meeting Date:_____

_____

Month 6 Meeting Date:_____

_____

End Date/Status: _____

APPENDIX G: PROGRAM COMPLETION

Below is a sample program assessment form:

20XX <Chapter Name>
MENTORSHIP PROGRAM ASSESSMENT

What activities did you find most useful during the Mentorship Program?

1)

2)

3)

4)

What are some aspects of the Mentorship Program you believe could be improved?

1)

2)

3)

4)

Additional Comments:

20XX <Chapter Name>
MENTORSHIP PROGRAM ASSESSMENT

Name: _____ Date: _____

Please fill out and return this assessment to <Mentorship Committee Member> by email or at the November chapter meeting.

The main activities in the 20XX <Chapter Name>Mentorship Program were:

- Application Form
- Meetings with Mentor/Mentee
- Pre-Meeting w/ Group
- Mentee/Mentor Group Meetings
- Speed Mentoring
- Mentorship Program Communications
- Training Session
- Final Meeting

For the overall program please circle the number that best matches your opinion about it:

	☹ ☺ ☺ ☺ ☹	
PROGRESS PACE too slow a pace	1　3　5　3　1	**PROGRESS PACE** too fast a pace
ORGANIZATION too unorganized	1　3　5　3　1	**ORGANIZATION** too inflexibly organized
VIEWS ACKNOWLEDGED too little acknowledgement of different perspectives	1　3　5　3　1	**VIEWS ACKNOWLEDGED** too much acknowledgement of different perspectives
DISCUSSION DURATION too little discussion	1　3　5　3　1	**DISCUSSION DURATION** too much discussion

Individual Goals and Objectives – Were your Individual Goals and Objectives met during the program? (Please list your goals)	☹ Strong No/NA	☺ Maybe	☺ Strong Yes
1.	1/NA	2　3　4	5
2.	1/NA	2　3　4	5
3.	1/NA	2　3　4	5

Program Overall Value		
RATE THE VALUE OF THE MENTORSHIP PROGRAM FOR YOU not much value	1　2　3　4　5	**RATE THE VALUE OF THE MENTORSHIP PROGRAM FOR YOU** a great deal of value

Here is an example of a SHRM Certificate of Recognition:

APPENDIX H: REFERENCE AREA

All of the sample emails and forms in this book are available for download here:

http://www.KnottedRoadPress.com/Mentorship-Book/

Use the following password to unlock the zip file:

Mentorship2014

GLOSSARY

CCP – Abbreviation for Certified Compensation Professional. The Certified Compensation Professional (CCP) designation is known throughout the total rewards community as a mark of expertise and excellence in the fundamentals of compensation. The CCP is earned after obtaining a passing score for all ten required exams.

EEOC Audit – Abbreviation for the Equal Employment Opportunity Commission. The EEOC is responsible for enforcing federal laws that make it illegal to discriminate against a job applicant or an employee because of the person's race, color, religion, sex (including pregnancy), national origin, age (40 or older), disability or genetic information. Through its administrative enforcement process, the Commission receives, investigates, and resolves charges of employment discrimination filed against private sector employers, employment agencies, labor unions, and state and local governments, including charges of systemic discrimination.

HR Case Studies – For the purposes of this book, the term HR case studies is used to describe the process of analyzing after the fact a real-life situation experienced by one of the HR professionals in the mentorship group to illustrate an interesting or unusual application of HR principles.

HRCI – Abbreviation for HR Certification Institute. The HR Certification Institute is a global leader in developing rigorous exams to demonstrate mastery and real-world application of forward-thinking HR practices, policies and principles. Since 1976, the Institute has awarded hundreds of thousands of HR credentials to highly accomplished HR professionals from around the world who have successfully passed these exams and uphold the highest standards of the HR profession.

HRCI Recertification Credit – All HR professionals who have earned one or more designation through HRCI (see above) must earn a specified number of credits every three years to maintain their certification in good standing. Recertification is the process of renewing one's certification. Recertification credits can be earned through continuing education, instruction, on-the-job experience, research and publishing, leadership and professional memberships.

LinkedIn – A business-oriented social networking service. Founded in December 2002 and launched in May 2003, it is mainly used for professional networking. As of June 2013, LinkedIn reported more than 259 million acquired users in more than 200 countries and territories.

MBTI – Abbreviation for the Myers-Briggs Type Indicator assessment test. The MBTI assessment is a psychometric questionnaire designed to measure psychological preferences in how people perceive the world and make decisions.

Mentor Quads – A way of describing the groups of four mentors who meet once per month during the LWHRA mentorship program. The groups are formed with a geographic basis, so the mentors can meet regularly to offer support to each other in dealing with issues related to supporting their mentees during the mentorship program.

Personal Branding – Personal branding is defined as the ongoing process of establishing a prescribed image or impression in the mind of others about an individual, group or organization. For the purposes of this book, it is used to describe one of the monthly mentee meeting topics. At that meeting the mentees learn about the value of establishing or improving their personal brand to further their career and increase their effectiveness in searching for a new job.

PHR – Abbreviation for Professional in Human Resources. The PHR demonstrates mastery of the technical and operational aspects of HR practices and U.S. laws and regulations. The professionally relevant credential is for the HR professional who focuses on program implementation, has a tactical/logistical orientation, is accountable to another HR professional within the organization and has responsibilities that focus on the HR department rather than the whole organization.

SHRM – Abbreviation for the Society for Human Resource Management. Founded in 1948, the Society for Human Resource Management (SHRM) is the world's largest HR membership organization devoted to human resource management. Representing more than 275,000 members in over 160 countries, the Society is the leading provider of resources to serve the needs of HR professionals and advance the professional practice of human resource management. SHRM has more than 575 affiliated chapters within the United States and subsidiary offices in China, India and United Arab Emirates.

Speed Mentoring – The process of a mentee conducting a short, focused conversation with each of the mentors prior to the pairing process at the beginning of the mentorship program. The purpose of these mini-interviews is for the mentees to get a first impression of all of the mentees in the mentorship program, and vice versa, for the purpose of selecting the person they want to be paired with for their 1:1 work during the mentorship program.

SPHR – Abbreviation for Senior Professional in Human Resources. The SHPR certification is recognized as a professionally relevant credential for those who have mastered the strategic and policy-making aspects of HR management in the United States. It is designed for the HR professional who plans, rather than implements, HR policy, focuses on the "big picture," has ultimate accountability in the HR department, has breadth and depth of knowledge in all HR disciplines and understands the business beyond the HR function and influences the overall organization.

WIIFM – Acronym for the phrase *What's In It For Me?* Originally used in sales and marketing to emphasize for salespeople the importance of knowing why people would buy their product or service. For the purposes of this book, it is used to describe why the mentorship committee should understand why people would apply to participate in the mentorship program.

INDEX

About Knotted Road Press

Knotted Road Press fiction specializes in dynamic writing set in mysterious, exotic locations.

Knotted Road Press non-fiction publishes autobiographies, business books, cookbooks, and how-to books with unique voices.

Knotted Road Press creates DRM-free ebooks as well as high-quality print books for readers around the world.

With authors in a variety of genres including literary, poetry, mystery, fantasy, and science fiction, Knotted Road Press has something for everyone.

Knotted Road Press
www.KnottedRoadPress.com

Made in the USA
Charleston, SC
22 January 2015